HIRING
BUILDERS
AND
PROFESSIONALS

D1144113

Which? Books are commissioned and
2 Marylebone Road, London NW1 4DF
Email: books@which.co.uk

Distributed by Littlehampton Book Se
Faraday Close, Durrington, Worthing,

British Library Cataloguing in Publicati
A catalogue record for this book is av

Portsmouth City Council		
C800413200		
Askews		20-May-2010
692.8		£9.99
		9781844900763

ISBN 978 1 84490 076 3

1 3 5 7 9 10 8 6 4 2

This book incorporates material from Getting the Best From Your Builder by Benjamin Mee, published by Which? Books in 2004.

The publishers would like to thank the Which? Legal Service for their help in the preparation of this book, and Kate Faulkner/Designs on Property for the material on HIPs on page 104.

Consultant Editor: Natalia Gameson
Project Editor: Rochelle Venables
Editor: Emma Callery
Designers: Sharon Johnston and Bob Vickers
Indexer: Lynda Swindells
Printed and bound by Charterhouse, Hatfield

Arctic Volume White is an elemental chlorine-free paper produced at Arctic Paper Hafrestroms AB in Åsensbruk, Sweden, using timber from sustainably managed forests. The mill is ISO14001 and EMAS certified, and has FSC certified Chain of Custody.

For a full list of Which? Books, please call 01903 828557, access our website at www.which.co.uk, or write to Littlehampton Book Services.

For other enquiries call 0800 252 100.

HIRING BUILDERS AND PROFESSIONALS

- *Get the job done without getting ripped off!*

CONTENTS

Section 3 focuses on miscellaneous traders, including car mechanics, drains specialists, locksmiths and removal firms, as well as shining a light on more obscure trades such as antique restoration, chimney sweeping and piano tuning. In the case of the latter three trades, which although still necessary are commonly perceived as being a little antiquated, public awareness of how these trades should be carried out is often limited, leaving anyone in need of their services sadly at the mercy of potential rogue traders.

If you follow all the steps outlined in this book but your job still hasn't been carried out satisfactorily, Section 4 will tell you how to take your complaint further. You can also find out what you should do if you need to take your complaint to court in the worst case scenario – if your trader or professional goes bankrupt, for example, or is unable or unwilling to resolve your problem.

1 BUILDERS AND CONTRACTORS

- Builders
- Carpenters and joiners
- Carpet fitters
- Fencers
- Gardeners, landscapers and tree surgeons
- Gas installers, plumbers and electricians
- Handymen
- Kitchen and bathroom fitters
- Painters and decorators
- Plasterers
- Roofers
- Window fitters

FINDING THE RIGHT CONTRACTOR FOR YOU

There are some jobs around the home that you can't – or don't want to – do yourself; jobs that may require specialist skills. Renovating your home in any way is generally regarded with dread by those who have never done it before, but also, more ominously, by those who have. Horror stories are common, and it is estimated that botched home improvements and shoddy repairs cost us well in excess of a billion pounds each year.

This section covers projects and jobs that are too big or complex to do yourself. It will help you plan what you need to do, establish whether you will need permission to do it, determine who you will need to hire – and what you should look for before hiring. After all, the fact that you're looking to employ a trader at all probably indicates that you don't know much about the job yourself. This can put you at a disadvantage, leaving you reliant on the trader to tell you what needs doing, how long it's going to take and how much it will cost.

But it doesn't have to be a task that you view with trepidation. With a bit of forward planning, things can swing back in your favour. So, to arm you with the information you need, we're taking a close look at the most popular trades to give you an idea of what to look for, what to expect, what to pay and what levels of service you should expect during the work – and after the job is finished.

You can never guarantee a perfect job, but you can significantly reduce your chances of hitting disaster by choosing a trader carefully, and by following a few simple steps. But even if you need a trader in an emergency, don't be tempted to go for the first or largest ad in your local paper. A little bit of homework could save you time, money and hassle in the long run.

Choosing and checking
BUILDERS

Anything that involves getting planning permission or interacting with building professionals, such as general builders, structural engineers or district surveyors, is best left to experienced professionals.

Consider checking Which? Local for builders in your area. Which? Local is a subscriber service that helps consumers find reliable tradespeople to carry out work in their homes. Local service providers, including builders, plumbers and gardeners, are recommended by members who have had direct experience of hiring them. Buy With Confidence (www.buywithconfidence.gov.uk) can help you find a trader who has been approved by Trading Standards, although at the time of writing its coverage is not yet country-wide. A good builder should also have NVQs or HNDs in construction, and should be able to show you copies of their certificates.

Check Which? Local for recommendations in your area, and obtain a number of references at this initial stage. Ask your builder for three phone numbers of satisfied customers who have had work done of a similar nature recently. Follow this up with phone calls to the referees and make sure you establish that the builder is courteous, capable of completing the job in hand on time, and reliable. Don't accept written references – these can easily be forged. The same applies to any trader you're looking to hire.

To check if your builder is financially secure, ask for the phone numbers of three frequently used suppliers, such as a brick manufacturer or a cement supplier, to check if your builder pays them on time, and how long they have to wait for payment.

Women-only firms or traders
If you're interested in working with female-only building businesses, it's worth visiting Women and Manual Trades (WAMT) online at www.wamt.org.

WAMT is the national organisation for tradeswomen and women working in trade. You can browse through their online directory of tradeswomen to find one working in your area. Bear in mind, however, that this isn't a registration scheme that vets the work of its members.

CARPENTERS AND JOINERS

Carpenters may specialise in different types of work, covering everything from building stud walls, floors and staircases, to fitting joists, kitchens and worktops.

Joiners differ from carpenters in that they will cut and fit joints in wood that don't use nails. They usually do this in a workshop environment since the formation of the various joints they are working on requires non-portable machinery. A carpenter will generally work on site.

Carpenters and joiners don't necessarily need any formal qualifications to practise, although some may have NVQ qualifications in, for example, wood occupations, levels one to three. Look for at least five years' experience in either discipline before hiring.

You can get details of qualified and experienced carpenters and joiners from the not-for-profit government body TrustMark at www.trustmark.org.uk. TrustMark claim that any approved trader has had their technical skills independently checked in regular on-site inspections, as well as their trading record and financial status.

CARPET FITTERS

It is possible to fit your own carpets and flooring, but as you're dealing with potentially very expensive materials, it is best to leave the job to the professionals. Many firms selling carpets will provide their own fitters, but if they don't, visit the National Institute of Carpet and Floor Layers at www.nicfltd.org.uk for a database of approved fitters. Members must have completed a written or oral examination and have supplied the details of three referees who can attest to the standard of their work.

For flooring, look out for a trader who has completed a course with the Flooring Industry Training Association (FITA).

FENCERS

If you're having fencing fitted in your garden, employing a professional fencing contractor would certainly make life easier than going down the DIY route. Traders will remove and dispose of your old fence, and advise on the best type of fence to suit your needs, whether this is timber, steel, aluminium, wire or PVC fencing.

The Fencing Contractors Association (FCA) has an online directory of accredited fencers in your area at www.fencingcontractors.org. FCA members have been vetted for reliability, experience, the quality of their work and comply with the FCA's code of conduct.

Most of the firms listed will provide all types of fencing, but if you need a more specialist trader, such as one to provide electric fencing, the FCA also incorporates the Electric Security Fencing Federation, the Gate Automation and Access Barrier Association and the Association of Safety Fencing Contractors.

GARDENERS, LANDSCAPERS AND TREE SURGEONS

Hiring a gardener can be a big investment, whether you're after a casual horticulturist or a specialist landscaper. Casual gardeners will be able to take on small tasks, such as mowing the lawn, weeding or cutting hedges and general maintenance. You can search for a gardener in a number of ways, going on recommendations from family or friends or on Which? Local. You can also post the job you need doing on online site www.myhammer.co.uk. Gardeners in your area will offer a range of quotations for the job, and you can check how they've been rated by past customers.

For more complicated jobs such as building a wall, laying a patio area or conducting a complete garden makeover, a landscaper gardener may be a more practical option.

Landscapers should belong to one of the two major trade associations: the British Association of Landscape Industries (BALI, www.bali.co.uk) or the

---

Qualifications matter
Arboricultural Association (AA) approved tree surgeons are not always more expensive, but even if they are, their services may prove a saving in the long run. A *Which? Gardening* survey (published in November 2002) found that AA contractors produced the most detailed and accurate assessments.

Association of Professional Landscapers (APL, www.landscaper.org.uk). Ask for the names and addresses of previous clients so you can check the quality and style of their work.

The main trade association for tree surgeons, who deal with everything from tree cutting to thinning and pruning, is the Arboricultural Association (AA, at www.trees.org.uk). Look to hire a tree surgeon with either a BTEC Diploma in forestry and arboriculture, an NVQ in arboriculture, or equivalent qualifications offered by the Royal Forestry Society. Get at least one quote from an AA approved contractor. Tree surgeons can also provide advice on maintenance requirements, planting, cable bracing, pest and disease control and the felling of trees in difficult positions.

GAS INSTALLERS, PLUMBERS AND ELECTRICIANS

Some trade bodies carry compulsory membership. Anyone working on gas appliances or installing a gas cooker must be a Gas Safe member – this replaced the CORGI system on 1 April 2009 – or work for British Gas. Ask for their registration number, which can be checked at the Gas Safe Register site at www.gassaferegister.co.uk.

Plumbers may also need to be Gas Safe registered if you're using one to install central heating, which means they must have passed a Certificate of Competence through an Accredited Certification scheme. They should also have the relevant NVQ qualifications – if they're running their own business, plumbers should really have attained NVQ Level 3. Check if they are a member

---

Do I need to hire an electrician?

Minor jobs that don't need to be carried out by a certified electrician or inspected include:

▶ Repairing or replacing fixed electrical equipment, such as plug sockets, switches, cables and ceiling roses.

▶ Adding extra power points, light fittings and switches to an existing circuit, unless they are outdoors or in rooms such as the kitchen or bathroom, where water is present.

of the Chartered Institute of Plumbing and Heating Engineering at www. ciphe.org.uk, which has around 12,000 members. For more information about plumbers' trade bodies, see page 145.

Electricians must be Part P qualified to carry out most electrical jobs, which means they must have completed a Building Regulations Part P Domestic Installers course, after which they should have registered with a Competent Person Self-Certification scheme, such as the one run by the National Inspection Council for Electrical Installation Contracting (NICEIC) . To check if your electrician is registered, visit www.competentperson.co.uk.

HANDYMEN

If you need help with odd jobs around the house, you might consider hiring a handyman or woman. But tread carefully, as they are most likely to be a sole trader who is not covered by a trade association. Make sure they have some experience in the sort of work you need doing and ask to see examples of their recent work, if possible. Request the phone numbers of at least three recent clients to make sure their work was of a professional standard.

You can search for handymen and women online on a number of websites. MyHammer.co.uk offers a free service on which you can post your jobs, and traders will respond to your advert with quotes – the site says it can save consumers as much as 30 per cent on jobs. Tradesmen listed on the site are also rated by former customers, so you can get an idea of the sort of person you'll be hiring beforehand in addition to some information on their skills. Visit www.myhammer.co.uk to post a job online.

KITCHEN AND BATHROOM FITTERS

Before hiring, consider that kitchen and bathroom fitters need to have a wide range of skills. Anyone fitting a built-in kitchen would need a thorough understanding of electrics and plumbing, in addition to carpentry skills, and fitting a gas cooker will require your trader to be Gas Safe registered. Certain electrical work must be carried out by a Part P registered electrician. If your fitter doesn't have these skills, you will need to employ separate people to carry out any specialist tasks, so check beforehand, although in reality, most fitters have received enough training in plumbing and electrical work to do the whole job.

The Kitchen Bathroom Bedroom Specialists Association (KBSA) is the main trade body for kitchen and bathroom fitters. You can search the KBSA's online directory to find an accredited member in your area at www.kbsa.org.uk. If you purchase a kitchen or bathroom from one of its members, you will be automatically covered by the KBSA's free ConsumerCare Deposit Protection Scheme, or the ConsumerCare Plus Scheme, which insures you against the loss of your deposit and other payments in case your trader goes bust, and offers a six-year warranty. You can find out more information on these schemes at www.kbsa.org.uk.

PAINTERS AND DECORATORS

Look to hire a professional who is a member of the Painting and Decorating Association (www.paintingdecoratingassociation.co.uk). Members must have been trading for at least a year, have had at least three references checked and be financially vetted.

PLASTERERS

Plasterwork relates to construction or ornamentation done with plaster, covering tasks from laying plaster on interior walls to shaping decorative moldings on ceilings and walls. If you're hiring a trader without a City and Guilds qualification or an NVQ, make sure you get at least three references from your plasterer's previous clients, and try to source one listed on the Federation of Plastering and Drywall Contractors website at www.fpdc.org.

Bear in mind that plastering is a separate trade in its own right – many believe the job can be done by decorators and painters, which isn't true unless they have the required level of skill to strengthen and seal the walls of your house against external conditions.

ROOFERS

It's best to get a specialist rather than a general builder to carry out roofing installation work because of the need to make the structure weatherproof as soon as possible. You can get the names of registered roofers from the National Federation of Roofing Contractors at www.nfrc.co.uk. Check that your potential roofer is licensed, certified, and has a number of years' experience in roofing installation.

If you're looking to hire someone to install a green roof, which partially or wholly covers over the surface area of your roof with vegetation and soil to absorb water, provide extra insulation or to create a habitat for wildlife, you may need to hire a landscaper. Visit the British Association of Landscape Industries (BALI, www.bali.co.uk) or the Association of Professional Landscapers (APL, www.landscaper.org.uk) to find a list of registered landscapers in your area.

Independent demonstration and research body, the Green Roof Centre, has an online directory of architects, installers, seed producers and substrate suppliers which you can search at www.greenroofcentre.co.uk.

To install solar panels, a number of firms have a trained network of installers. Solarcentury, for example, trained over 60 roofers across the UK in 2008 and 2009 to install solar electric roof tiles, and are continuing to train more. Visit www.solarcentury.co.uk to find an installer in your area.

WINDOW FITTERS

As with carpets and flooring, many firms that sell windows and double glazing will often provide their own fitters. Find out if the firm is Fenestration Self-Assessment Scheme (FENSA) accredited, as this is the body that governs the specification and installation of double glazing. To find a FENSA installer in your area, visit www.fensa.org.uk.

The Glass and Glazing Federation (GGF) is the equivalent trade association for fitting replacement windows, doors, energy efficient windows, conservatories, solar panels and more, although it, too, covers double glazing. All firms listed at the GGF's website, www.ggf.co.uk, are vetted and work to a Code of Good Practice.

What should you ask before hiring?

There are four key areas that you should always consider before hiring a builder or contractor:

Quotations: Before hiring any trader, try to pin them down to providing a total cost quotation, which should include material costs and labour time. Do not pay the total cost upfront, however, but enquire as to how much of a deposit you will be expected to pay. Establish whether VAT is included in the total price or whether you will have to pay that on top. Make sure your trader has an idea of your budget and how far it will stretch.

Waste materials: Find out who will take away waste materials at the end of the job and whether there will be an extra charge for this. Ensure that the materials you are paying your traders to use are good quality, to guard against being ripped off by tradesmen using lower quality materials than what you have paid for, and ask to see examples before work commences.

Complaints: It is a good idea to ask how your trader would deal with a complaint. There is so much potential for error in building work that it's important to establish before hiring that your trader will be willing to resolve any problems that may occur, or fix any faults or defects promptly in the finished work. You can request a referral from a former job that involved a complaint to see how it was dealt with.

Insurance: Any trader you employ must have adequate insurance to cover the following:
▶ Accidental damage to your home.
▶ Accidental damage to adjoining properties.
▶ Personal injury or public liability insurance to the trader and their staff.
Ensure that any subcontractors used are covered by the main contractor's policy for damage or injury.

BUILDERS

As building work is likely to involve larger sums of cash than other home improvements, it is crucial to make as many checks as possible and ask lots of questions before breaking ground on your project. According to a Which? survey, builders caused more problems for consumers than any other trade, with nearly 40 per cent of respondents experiencing problems with their builders.

Find out what specific experience the builder has in doing the sort of work you want before hiring. It's important to see recent examples of the builder's work, especially if you want a large job doing, such as an extension.

The Federation of Master Builders (FMB) will be able to provide you with examples of builders with particular specialisms, such as extensions. Visit www.fmb.org.uk to search their online directory. If you're commissioning a two- or three-storey structure, it's vital to use a builder with experience in this area.

Ask the builder to come with you to meet the people who own the property whose work you're inspecting. Don't accept a written reference – these can very easily be faked.

Ask how long their waiting list is for new clients. A good builder may be booked up for more than a year ahead and will always be busy. It may be worth waiting to get the best man for the job. Be flexible in your work schedule, rather

---

Cowboys: spotting the signs

Rogue traders can come across as polite, charming and professional. Watch out for the following signs, which should set alarm bells ringing:

▶ Uninvited calls offering to do work in your home.
▶ No contract is offered, or the trader won't sign one that you give to them.
▶ Quotes are handwritten and don't give much detail.
▶ Your trader only provides a mobile number as his/her point of contact, and offers no other addresses or contact numbers.
▶ Your trader never gives his/her company name when answering the phone.
▶ A discount is offered for cash, and money is requested upfront.
▶ They refuse to give you references or show you previous work they've done.

Trust your instincts. If you have any initial doubts, it's best to look elsewhere.

Building Regulations

The Building Regulations, created under the Building Act 1984, detail how you carry out building work to your home across England and Wales, regardless of whether or not planning permission is required. In Scotland, the Building Regulations that apply were set out in the Building (Scotland) Act 2003.

Building Regulations are enforced by your local authority's Building Regulations department, and is generally known in the trade as building control. Depending on the nature of your work, you will be sending in either a Full Plans application, or a Building Notice (see page 40 for more information).

The Building Act allows for building control to be exercised by an independent approved inspector who you can hire. You can find one operating in your area online or in the Yellow Pages, or searching the online directory of trade association the Association of Consultant Approved Inspectors (ACAI) at www.approvedinspectors. org.uk.

However, the vast majority of work is still handled by local authority building control officers (BCOs), or building inspectors as they are sometimes known. A BCO will be appointed to your project after you have received Building Regulations approval for your project. You will be charged for both services.

With a few exceptions – conservatories and porches, for example – everything that affects the health and safety of the people living in your home must meet the requirements of the Building Regulations. These are also concerned with energy conservation and with establishing a means of escape in the event of a fire, and cover access for the disabled.

The Regulations tend to only give general requirements. How they are interpreted in practice is up to the BCO involved. Visit the Government's website on Building Regulations at www.communities.gov.uk to download the 13 Approved Documents, which give guidance on how to meet the functional requirements of the regulations.

Any builder you employ must have a thorough understanding of the latest Building Regulations. Sit down with your builder and the local BCO, if applicable, at the start of your project to run through the plans. During a meeting like this, it will be pretty obvious if your builder doesn't understand the latest regulations.

than going for someone you are unsure about but who fits in with your exact timetable. Going for the latter option could easily be a false economy.

Key questions:
▶ *How much experience do you have in the type of work I need doing?*
▶ *Can you show me at least three recent examples of your work?*

CARPENTERS AND JOINERS

It is important to make sure that you choose a carpenter or joiner with experience in the type of work you want done – for example, someone who specialises in building cupboards may not have the necessary skills to do major building work. So it's important to know exactly what you want before you hire anyone to make sure they will be specialised enough to fulfil your requirements.

It might even be a good idea to have a look at previous work they may have completed so that you can be doubly sure it's what you want. If this isn't possible, ask if they have a photographic portfolio of former work to show you, but make sure before hiring that you have some evidence they will be able to meet your needs.

Key questions:
▶ *How much experience do you have in this type of work?*
▶ *Do you have a portfolio of past work that I can look at?*

CARPET FITTERS

If you are hiring your own carpet fitter, obtain the usual references and recommendations. Find out exactly what your quotation covers – if you're buying your carpet from a shop, will you need to pay the fitter on the day, if they don't work for the shop directly and, if so, how much would this cost? Is VAT included or on top of costs? Will there be any additional costs on material, such as for special glue to fit the carpet? Ask the company to give you an estimated fitting time on the day you've agreed for the fitting to take place – morning or afternoon – to avoid having to wait in all day. The same principles apply to choosing a flooring fitter.

Key questions:
▶ *What does the quotation I've been given cover? Will there be any additional costs?*
▶ *Can you give me an estimated time for the fitting on the day we've agreed?*

FENCERS

Obtain the usual references and referrals from past clients and at Which? Local. Fence installation is a competitive industry, so you should find it easy to obtain at least three quotes for your work.

Ask if the company offers any kind of warranty, and determine what their response time will be. Fence fitters tend to have lots of clients, so you may be waiting for a while before they can do your work.

Key questions:
▶ *How long will it take you to do the job?*
▶ *Do you offer a warranty for the finished product?*
▶ *If so, how long will it last for?*

GARDENERS, LANDSCAPERS AND TREE SURGEONS

Take extra care here as gardeners you're looking to hire may be sole traders who are not covered by a trade association code of conduct. This means you will have less hope of tracking them down or putting things right if there's a problem. In this case, it's vital to get recommendations if you can, and ask to see examples of former work to check it will fit your requirements.

Pinning down an exact quotation is sometimes difficult with gardeners and landscapers. When *Which? Gardening* investigated landscape gardeners in July 2004, it found that many didn't return calls or turn up to give quotes, so you may need to call quite a few before finding the right gardener for the job. Many quotes were found to be vague, and traders often failed to supply details about the quantity or type of materials to be used. Others were unclear about the work that needed to be done, while some didn't take the needs and suggestions of the owners into consideration. Insist on receiving a detailed and thorough quote – this is vital in case things go wrong.

Is your tree protected?

Your tree surgeon should be able to advise on any trees in your garden which may need protecting – be suspicious if they seem clueless on this issue. Some trees are protected by local planning authorities (LPAs), usually a branch of your local council, and any unauthorised work, even the pruning of branches on a preserved tree, can result in a hefty fine. Your trees may also be protected if your home lies within a conservation area. Merely cutting off a branch from a tree with a tree preservation order (TPO) on it without gaining permission first could result in a fine of £2,500, and chopping a tree down could land you with a bill of £20,000.

It's crucial before beginning your work to contact your LPA or tree officer to check on the status of a tree, and if necessary, to apply for an application form to carry out your work. It won't stand up in court when you're fined to plead that you were unaware a TPO existed on a particular tree, unless your LPA failed to give you the right information. You can download more guidance notes on making an application for tree works from www.planningportal.gov.uk.

If there is a special tree in your garden, road, or even in your neighbour's garden that you'd like to protect, it's possible to apply to have a TPO served on it. Contact your LPA by phone – for particularly important trees that are under immediate threat, a TPO can be served on the same day.

Make sure you find out if there is a condition attached to the original planning permission for your property that restricts the planting of trees or hedges by contacting your local authority. Get your landscape gardener's home number and address so they can't just disappear if things go awry.

Tree surgeons are more rigorously policed as they are answerable to the Arboricultural Association. Ensure you get the usual recommendations, and establish at the outset what will be included in your quote. Tree surgery can be very messy, so it's important to know if they will be clearing up the debris when the job is finished.

Also enquire if any trees in your garden are protected by local planning authorities (LPAs), usually the council to which you pay your Council Tax, under a Tree Protection Order (TPO). Your local council will be able to provide you with this information, and provide you with an application form for tree works if your tree is protected (see box above).

Key questions:
▶ *Can you provide me with a detailed and thorough quote?*
▶ *Do you understand the implications of doing work on a tree that is protected or has a TPO on it?*

GAS INSTALLERS, PLUMBERS AND ELECTRICIANS

Before hiring a gas installer, plumber or electrician, check their hourly charge-out rate, and ask them how long the job will take so you have an idea of the total cost. Make sure you find out if they will be adding on call-out fees, which can bump up a reasonable hourly rate. Be wary of tradespeople who charge more for the first hour, too. Get a range of quotes to obtain the best overall price for the job.

Bear in mind that an electrician may need to cut holes in your walls, depending on what work is being done. They won't be responsible for this damage, unless it can be shown that they have been negligent and fallen below the standard of a reasonable competent electrician, doing that particular job. So before the job starts, ask about how much potential harm may be caused to your property as a result of the work. Check if the electrician is bringing assistants along if the job is quite large, and how much more they will add onto your bill to cover this cost. Remember that the electrician who you employ is liable for any work that is subcontracted.

Make sure you obtain the usual references, and check Which? Local for recommendations.

Key questions:
▶ *Can you give me a written exact and firm quotation for the total cost?*
▶ *If not, what is your total estimate of the job's costs?*
▶ *Will you be using extra members of staff when carrying out the work, and will I be paying extra for this?*

HANDYMEN

If you're using a sole trader, it is vital to get references and recommendations by either word of mouth, or by getting an online review from Which? Local at www.which-local.co.uk. Describe the job you'd like them to take on, and get at least three quotes from different traders. Find out straight away how they'd like to be paid – some may prefer cash, but others will accept cheques or payment by BACS. If they do want to be paid in cash, ask for proof from past accounts that they have declared this on their annual self-assessment tax return.

Make sure you have a home number for your handyperson, and an address too, so your trader can't just disappear if things go wrong. Find out how many clients they have already, and whether they will be able to fit you in easily, or if you will be waiting for weeks for their services.

Key questions:
▶ *How long is your waiting list?*
▶ *What type of payment do you accept for your work?*

KITCHEN AND BATHROOM FITTERS

A Which? survey found that only 63 per cent of Which? readers were satisfied with the service provided by their kitchen or bathroom fitter – one of the lowest satisfaction figures in the survey.

So, take these steps to make sure you are satisfied with the final product. Ask to see a couple of examples of kitchens the firm you have highlighted may have fitted in the area recently, and ask for the phone numbers of past clients to find out how courteous the fitters were throughout the job. Did they clean up at the end of the day, and were they understanding about helping their clients to continue living around their workspace?

Is the timing going to be right for both of you? Will your trader be able to work around the delivery of your new suite so that you're not left with sorting out the storage of this before they can start work?

Key questions:
▶ *Can I see photos of kitchens/bathrooms you've fitted recently?*
▶ *Will you be able to start work on my kitchen/bathroom as soon as my new fixtures/appliances are delivered?*

Sustainable microgeneration and products

Small home microgeneration is an umbrella term covering the installation of solar panels, ground source heat pumps, solar thermal systems and micro turbines. The Microgeneration Scheme lists on its website a series of reputable installers and products for these new and emerging sustainable technologies. The scheme is backed by the Government and supported by the Energy Saving Trust. Visit www.microgenerationcertification.org for a list of suppliers in your area.

If you're looking to install heat pumps, ensure you use a registered plumbing and heating professional. Visit the Chartered Institute of Plumbing and Heating Engineering website to find registered professionals at www.ciphe.org.uk, then follow this checklist before commissioning any work:

▶ Ensure you outline your requirements immediately with your trader, and find out which products might be suitable for your home.

▶ Ask what benefits each product has, including energy and water savings and environmental advantages. Find out how long the payback period will be for your outlay.

▶ Find out if any further work is necessary to ensure maximum efficiency for your new system – will you need any extra insulation to improve the thermal efficiency of the building?

▶ Will the work require Building Regulations approval and certification?

▶ Are there any grants available to offset the cost of the work? Visit www.government-grants.co.uk to see what you might qualify for.

When commissioning more general green work, such as installing extra insulation or a new boiler, the Energy Institute has an online register of energy consultants for view at www.energyinst.org.uk. Each consultant registered with the institute must meet minimum standards of competence, experience and qualifications, and maintain good levels of continuing professional development to join. Choosing an installer from here also gives you a valuable forum to turn to if anything goes wrong with your new sustainable products, or the technology you commissioned to be fitted doesn't meet your requirements.

A number of firms have now also set up as sustainable consultancies that can advise on what technology will best complement your home, or put right any damage where homeowners have installed inappropriate green technology which doesn't work as efficiently as expected. Conneco is one example, and charges £250 plus travel costs for a home visit, and a subsequent report. Visit www.conneco.org.uk for more information.

PAINTERS AND DECORATORS

In our Which? survey, 70 per cent of respondents said they were very happy with the work done by their painter/decorator. But a quarter reported problems. Timing was often the main issue – jobs tended to take a lot longer than the painter/decorator had originally estimated.

Show your painter/decorator the rooms before they supply a quote, and ask them to estimate how long the job will take. Avoid using firms or sole traders who charge for quotes.

If you need the job done by a certain date, ask the painter if he can do it by this date. If he says that he can, then make 'time of the essence' a condition of the contract. By making 'time of the essence' a condition of the contract, if the painter is unable to finish on the date agreed, then you will be able to terminate the contract and instruct another painter to finish the job, charging the cost to the original painter.

Key questions:
▶ *How long will the job take in total?*
▶ *Does your quote include the cost of materials?*

PLASTERERS

Follow the usual route of obtaining a list of former clients and references, or following recommendations from friends and family. As the costs of plastering vary according to your area and the plasterer's level of experience, get a few quotes in hand before commissioning any work.

Again, be wary of traders who charge for quotes, or who will charge you by the hour for their labour, as this gives them little incentive to do the job quickly.

Some plasterers may have only worked in new buildings, so if you are looking to have plaster repair work done without removing the old plaster, then you'll need to ensure you are employing a trader with enough experience in this field.

Key questions:
▶ *Can you give me a written exact and firm quotation for the total cost?*
▶ *If not, what is your total estimate of the job's costs?*
▶ *Do you have experience of plastering new/older properties?*

ROOFERS

Ask your roofer to provide a list of former clients and references, and say you'd like to see examples of their work.

Find out how much of a deposit will be payable upfront, and ask for a written quotation of the estimated final costs.

Ask when you will be provided with guarantees and manufacturers' warranties. Will your roofer be obtaining the required re-roofing building permits? You will need to obtain these from your LPA before carrying out any serious changes to your roof. Be wary of anyone who is unsure of what these are, or unwilling to do this.

Ask how long your trader has been installing and repairing roofs for – look for five years at a minimum – and check they have experience in working with roofs similar to yours.

If you own a thatched roof, it is crucial to hire an experienced thatcher. Check Which? Local for recommendations.

Key questions:
▶ *How much experience do you have in roof repair and installation?*
▶ *Can you provide me with a full quote upfront?*

WINDOW FITTERS

Double glazing companies don't always enjoy good press – our Which? survey found that only 63 per cent of respondents were satisfied with the service they received.

If you receive an unsolicited call, it's wise to quickly follow this up with a reference request.

Be wary of companies that go for the hard sell. A common problem with many double glazing companies is their sales technique, so if you feel pressurised or unsure in any way about the products you are buying, say you need time to think about it. Remember, you are under no obligation to buy, even if you've let the salesperson into your house. Remember that the Consumer Protection from Unfair Trading Regulations 2007 contains prohibitions against misleading and aggressive practices. So if you feel that means of harassment, coercion or undue influence were used, contact your local Trading Standards.

Get all quotations they provide in writing, and refuse to sign up immediately. It's also worth checking if the window fitters the company is using are contracted or employed by the firm. It could make a difference to the quality of the work they produce if the fitters are paid per day or per job – if it is the latter, they may be tempted to rush your job to get on with their next appointment.

If the company's salesman starts telling you how bad their competitors are, it's time to ask them to leave. Under the Glass and Glazing Federation rules, they are prohibited from doing this.

Key questions:
▶ *Can you provide a full quotation in writing?*
▶ *Are the fitters you employ paid a set rate, or one that's calculated according to the number of jobs they carry out each day?*

What legal issues should you be aware of?

Generally, small-scale home improvements only need a letter of agreement to set out a contract. It needs to be signed by both parties, and should cover and include the following points:
▶ A brief description of the job to be done.
▶ The agreed price for the work, with a copy of the contractor's original quotation attached to the back of the letter.
▶ The name of the person responsible for obtaining any necessary official approval for the work.
▶ The agreed start and finish dates. The phrase 'time is of the essence' should be included if meeting the finishing date is important.
▶ A requirement that the trader should leave the site in a tidy state at the end of the work.
▶ A clause detailing whether any part of the payment can be withheld in the event of a dispute arising between the parties, or on completion of the job, as a retainer against the cost of rectifying any defects found in the work.
▶ Any special instructions regarding what aspect of the work you would like to be carried out first.

▸ A requirement that any changes to the specification are to be confirmed in writing.

▸ A requirement that the contractor must be properly insured.

▸ The total cost of the work and how it will be paid – a lump sum at the end or stage payments as the work progresses.

▸ A clause stating that the wages of any subcontractors employed by your trader are his/her responsibility. Don't agree to pay any subcontractors directly.

▸ A requirement that the contractor returns to put right any defects in the work, and any damage caused to your property, at the contractor's expense.

▸ If you have taken out an insurance backed guarantee (IBG, see overleaf), include the details here.

For an example of the type of contract you will need to draw up, you can download a series of free contracts on the FMB's website at www.fmb.org.uk.

But there are many other things to consider and clarify before you allow ground to break on your project.

ARE THEY INSURED?

Check your trader is appropriately insured before hiring. Ask to see copies of their insurance certificates, and make sure they don't expire during your project. Your trader should have the following insurance:

▸ Public liability insurance in case someone gets hurt on your site.

▸ Cover in case there is damage to your property, so that they can redo the work, or are insured to pay others to clean up their mess, such as decorators who may be required to cover up any marks left by a poor plastering job.

▸ Cover in case the builder goes bust, or has an accident, so you can pay someone else to finish the job for you.

Ask to see copies of your trader's indemnity policy documents. If insurance details are stated in your quotation, you should be covered. If your trader is going to employ subcontractors, it's a good idea to make sure that they hold proper insurance too, so that you aren't held liable for any accidents that may happen on the job.

IS THEIR WORK COVERED BY AN INSURANCE BACKED GUARANTEE?

Check your trader has an insurance backed guarantee (IBG) before employing them. Even the best trader occasionally goes bust through no fault of their own, or is unable to complete the job due to ill health or an accident. This can be difficult for everyone involved when you have laid out large sums of money and there is rain coming in through a hole where your roof used to be.

It is important to distinguish between these schemes and traders who simply advertise 'all work guaranteed'. This gives you no protection if your trader goes bankrupt. You may find that you are covered for the completion of unfinished . work if your trader is a member of a trade association, but you should notify the association first before work starts to be accepted for cover.

QUOTATIONS AS CONTRACTS

Some contractors, certainly in the case of window and double glazing suppliers, conservatory installers and kitchen and bathroom fitters, will supply quotations that are detailed enough to act as contracts. These may have the contractor's standard terms and conditions printed on the back of the quotation.

Read the terms very carefully before you sign on the dotted line – they are often more for the supplier's benefit than yours, and once you have signed the document, you are legally bound by them.

An exception to this is in the case of contracts for replacement windows and new kitchens that are ordered in specific circumstances. If a seller makes either a solicited or unsolicited call at your home, or visits you by appointment after making a phone call, and you place an order for goods during their visit, you have some rights of cancellation, even if you have signed a contract. These are as follows:

▶ Written notice of your rights must be given to you when you sign the order. If it isn't, the seller can't enforce the contract.

▶ You then have a 'cooling-off' period of seven days, during which time you can cancel the order by writing to the seller. Any deposit you paid when you signed the order must be returned to you in full.

Check thoroughly if your products come with guarantees, and get evidence of this in writing.

IBG providers

These bodies offer insurance backed guarantees:

▶ The Building Guarantee Scheme (BGS) sponsored by the Construction Employers Federation (CEF) covers work between £500 and £250,000 in Northern Ireland and England. The guarantee also covers any additional costs of completing faulty work to the value of £15,000, and gives a six-month defects liability period, followed by a two-year period of cover for any structural defects. You can search the CEF's online directory for a list of BGS registered builders at www.cefni.co.uk.

▶ The Federation of Master Builders (FMB) provides an IBG in the form of a MasterBond warranty. There are several levels of cover available under the MasterBond, ranging from two- to ten-year insurance cover periods, which cover an 'all risks' element, and guarantee varying periods of structural protection. You can source a MasterBond registered builder in an online directory on the FMB's website at www.fmb.org.uk.

▶ Homepro Insurance offers a range of flexible IBGs. If your contractor ceases to trade after he/she has received your deposit, then the money you have paid out will be recovered under the policy. This only applies if work hasn't started on site, however, and under a maximum period of 90 days from the date when your contractor first received the deposit. Depending on what type of policy you've taken out, you could also claim on it against the guarantee for faulty workmanship or materials, and the policy will provide for an approved contractor to remedy the work. This guarantee period can last up to ten years on most home improvements, although the policy you have will need to back the guarantee provided by your trader – if your trader will guarantee his/her work for five years, so will the policy.

▶ Quality Assured National Warranties (QANW) offer IBGs for window and door installers, and on cement repairs, decking, general building, roofing, extensions and conversions and underpinning. Guarantees range between cover periods of one year and ten years. Visit www.qanw.co.uk for more information.

▶ Installations Assured (IA) insure trades such as kitchen and bathroom suppliers, electricians and most other home improvement traders. Visit www.iaibg.co.uk.

BUILDING CONTRACTS

Building contracts are often complex documents. The builder should provide a contract for their services, detailing the schedule of payment related to progress, a start and end date, arrangements for possession of the site, insurance and variations or changes to the works. The contract may cover not just the employment of a builder, but also a contract administrator, whether that's an architect or a surveyor.

Make sure to stipulate the sum of the total fee in your contract, plus the frequency and conditions of payments, such as the amount of work that should be completed before payment is due and, in the event of defective work, the amount of retention money, usually 5 per cent, which won't be paid until any problems are rectified.

Be wary of any builders who try to cap the amount of time you'll have to raise any defects with them, as this affects your statutory rights.

Contracts for major work should also include the tender drawings, the specification — usually a written brief from an architect or an engineer outlining the precise nature of the work that is to be carried out — and the materials that will be used.

The contract should also address the procurement of materials and supply of goods.

Green building works

If you're having any sustainable improvements made, there are even more things to consider putting in your contract. Make sure you specify exactly what you want in your brief, which may cover the following:

▶ Specify wastage limitations in your work, to ensure your builder will use all materials wisely. It's worth checking how your builder will offload any waste products.

▶ Outline your requirements for your builder to reuse and recycle materials where appropriate.

▶ Make sure your builder is aware of what sustainable materials you want them to supply and use in the building work.

The Joints Contracts Tribunal offers a series of standard building and design contracts. Visit www.jctltd.co.uk to find out more.

Don't risk undertaking a building project with only an oral contract in place. Seek professional advice from a solicitor if you are in any doubt about the terms of the contract, or you could wind up with a dispute about unfulfilled expectations.

If you're in any further doubt, contact the Joint Contracts Tribunal (JCT). The JCT produces standard forms of contracts and guidance notes for the construction industry, and is the most commonly used supplier of contracts to the building trade and its customers. Visit the JCT website at www.jctltd.co.uk.

GUARANTEES

Ideally, your builder will guarantee his/her work for a period of time, although you will also need to negotiate a timeframe when the work is completed within which they will rectify any faults you may find in their work – a year, for example. It is imperative to get this in writing as soon as possible. Check whether your builder will come back and do any necessary remedial work, or whether you could get someone else to do it under the guarantee.

PLANNING THE PROJECT

B efore you begin work on your project, it's important to do your homework thoroughly and have a good idea of what you want before you start. If you make any impractical or costly decisions, you may have to change some of your ideas to ones that are easier to implement further down the line. Even if compromise becomes inevitable, having a firm idea of the end point in your mind can stop the project from sliding into something unrecognisable from your original plan.

Some difficulties you may run into can be anticipated. If you are doing work on a run-down or old property, it's advisable to have damp, woodworm and rot surveys carried out to prevent unpleasant surprises later on. Will you need to find out about soil conditions or where the drains run? These are questions for an architect or a surveyor (see Section 2).

To meet any unforeseen difficulties that may crop up, keep back a contingency sum of between 10 and 20 per cent of the cost of the work to meet unexpected costs. Tell your trader that you have this sum stashed away, which they will be able to access, if necessary, with your permission. If you own an older property, where improvement works can attract an even greater number of unexpected costs, the sum you may need could be as much as 30 per cent of your basic budget.

Make sure your trader is aware of your exact budget when specifying the sort of products you would like to be used. Plan and itemise your spending carefully and well in advance.

Green gains
Ask your trader about whether the work they are doing can improve the energy efficiency of your home. A higher rating on your energy performance certificate (EPC) should mean lower bills, and may, in the future, make your home easier to sell.

Planning permission

After you've pinpointed the trader of your choice, make sure first of all that the work that you are looking to have done is exempt from planning permission by checking with your local authority.

You're likely to need planning permission if you wish to do any of the following:

▶ Extend your home upwards or forwards.
▶ Build extensions of more than a certain size.
▶ Change the use of your home in any way, including converting it into flats.

If you are in any doubt about whether you need to apply for planning permission, then contact your council's planning department immediately. You can search for your local council at: www.direct.gov.uk. If you're discovered to have done any work without the prior necessary approval, your council has the power to make you apply for permission retrospectively, or worse, issue an enforcement notice asking you to restore your home to its former condition or former use. If you disregard this, you could be fined or prosecuted, and may have to witness the extension you put up being demolished by bulldozers, whose services you will have paid for with your own taxes.

Note that an enforcement notice has to be issued within four years of the work being completed, or it cannot be legally enforced, unless the building is listed. Download the government guide *Planning: A Guide for Householders* at www. communities.gov.uk, and go through it with your builder.

APPLYING FOR PLANNING PERMISSION

If it turns out that you do, in fact, need to gain planning permission before breaking ground on your new project, contact the planning department of your local authority and ask for an application form. They will tell you their fee, and how many copies of the form you will need to send back.

Before you apply, seek advice from a planning consultant or building surveyor who could help you with the application of the plans. Builders can provide this service, but they will often tell you to consult a surveyor first. An advantage in using a local surveyor is that they will be familiar with the criteria adopted by the local planning authority. This may well save you the disappointment and costs of a refusal or possible changes that you will have to make.

Exemptions from planning permission

The following improvements and additions to your home should be exempt in England and Wales:

▶ A conservatory, providing it is under 30 square metres.

▶ Domestic TV and radio aerials, although you may need permission for some satellite dishes. Check with your local council.

▶ Extensions, which include conservatories and garages closer than 5 metres to your house, will be allowed as long as they don't increase the volume of the house by more than your 'permitted development rights'. These are also known as permitted developments (PDs), and dictate the changes you can make to your home without planning permission. Permitted development rights were extended in the Town and Country Planning (General Permitted Development) (Amended) (No. 2) (England) Order 2008 in October 2008, but the changes won't necessarily apply if you live in a conservation area. Visit www.planningportal.gov.uk for more information.

▶ Patios and areas of your garden that you would like to pave over are exempt as a rule. However, you may now need permission to pave over your front garden, as the Government are looking to regulate householders in this area in order to protect against floods. You won't need planning permission if your new driveway uses porous surfacing to allow the water to drain through, but if the surface that needs covering is more than 5 square metres, you will need to lay traditional, impermeable driveways that don't control rainwater run-off.

▶ Neither will you need planning permission to install garden sheds, homes for your pets, greenhouses, summer houses, ponds or swimming pools.

Building Regulations approval may be required for some works, such as a loft or basement conversion. This can be obtained from your local council. Ask if your trader will be sorting this out, or if you will need to apply for it yourself (see overleaf for more information).

Normally, you should make a full application, but you could also make an outline planning application – this is not detailed planning permission, but is a general application to show that, in theory, it will be possible to extend or work on your home in the future. This is a good way to find out what your local authority thinks of your idea before making any detailed plans.

After acknowledging your application, your council will place it on the planning register, where it can be inspected by any interested parties. The council may also notify your neighbours or put up a notice on or near your house outlining the prospective changes.

The application should be decided within eight weeks, although the process can take considerably longer. The council must decide whether there are

---

Building Regulations and local building control officers

Most small-scale home improvement projects don't warrant the employment of an architect, surveyor or other professional adviser, but may need to meet the requirements of the Building Regulations. This is where local building control officers (BCOs) come into the equation. They will give advice on what the Building Regulations require, and carry out site inspections if necessary during the project. Check with your local authority to see if this will be necessary, or make an appointment with your building control department.

When planning your building project, you can submit a full plans application to your local authority, or give a building notice to their building control service, depending on the amount and the type of work you're commissioning. A full plans application, better suited to larger projects, should contain plans showing all details of the construction process well in advance of when work will start on site. Your local authority will check your plans and consult any appropriate departments, such as fire and sewerage. They should come back to you with a decision in five weeks.

If your plans fit in with the Building Regulations, you will receive a notice stating that they have been approved. You may be asked to make changes or provide more details, or your local authority could come back to you with conditional approval, in which they'll specify modifications that could or should be made to your plans. If they are rejected, your local authority will explain why in their feedback.

Plans approval notices are valid for three years from the date on which you sent the plans in.

A buildings notice is ideal for smaller projects, and is similarly obtained from your local council. You won't have to prepare any plans for inspection, but your work will be inspected by your local BCO as it progresses. A buildings notice is also valid for three years from the date it was issued, and you need to give your council 48 hours' notice to obtain one before breaking ground on your work.

any good planning reasons for refusing consent – it won't reject your project simply because people oppose it. They may approve it in full, reject it or grant permission with conditions attached.

When permission is granted, you must start work within the specified time limit. Building control will issue a final certificate once you've gained permission, as well as a building control approval certificate, known as a Notice of Passing of Plans. If the construction doesn't comply with the Regulations, you will be prosecuted.

Types of building work

Whether you're changing the way you use existing rooms, rearranging existing rooms, adapting existing unused space, such as with a loft or basement conversion, or extending your room, you're going to need to have a firm idea of what you'd like to be done from the outset. This will help you to advise your builder on the type of work you'd like to be carried out. You should also come up with some alternative ideas in case your builder says the project you have in mind is unworkable.

CHANGING THE WAY YOU USE EXISTING ROOMS

Every room in your home has its own specific function. However, they need not stay that way if it doesn't suit you. You could discuss doing the following with your builder:
▶ Turning the main living room into a large kitchen-diner, and using your dining room and kitchen as separate rooms.
▶ Stripping out the built-in kitchen units you don't need to create extra space for a dining area.
▶ Fitting out your boxroom as a second bedroom.

REARRANGING EXISTING ROOMS

Changing the layout of your home is a bit more radical than rearranging rooms. There are several options you could consider:

▶ Creating fewer and larger rooms by knocking down internal walls. Making an open-plan living-and-dining room or kitchen is one popular option. Upstairs, you could convert two bedrooms into one large master bedroom.

▶ Do you want to change the position of existing doors? An outside door in a kitchen could provide a useful route out to the bin or garden, for example.

▶ Changing the size of adjacent rooms by moving a partition wall and re-erecting it to provide one larger and one smaller room.

▶ Creating smaller rooms by installing new partitions in large existing rooms, or erecting new partitions to divide up floor space.

Ask your builder for his/her opinion on ways in which you could alter your existing space.

ADAPTING UNUSED SPACE

If you're looking to do a loft or basement conversion, you could convert these unused areas into new living space without building out your home.

Loft conversions are one of the most popular large-scale home improvements. Your builder should be able to advise on how feasible a conversion will be, to make sure that the roof structure won't be weakened by any conversion work. Planning permission isn't generally required.

When it comes to basement conversions, get your builder to check for damp, ventilation and lack of natural light to check if the conversion is possible. Converting a basement may be simple if the rooms are free from damp, but the job can become much more complex and expensive if you intend to use it as an habitable room.

EXTENSIONS

Decide on the type of extension you would like, and ask your builder for advice. If you need more bedrooms or an extra bathroom, you may need a two-storey extension, which will make matters increasingly complicated. Make sure you know exactly what you will be using the extra space for. Do you need an extra bedroom, a play room or a study? This will also affect the total cost and help you to budget early on – if you're installing an extra bathroom, for example, the amount of traders you will need to employ will increase, as plumbers and bathroom fitters will become part of the equation.

When planning your extension, you may need to seek advice from an architect and a surveyor (see Section 2). You should aim to match your extension to the original design of your house – if you own an older property that is listed or live in a conservation area, check if it's compulsory to use local stone to build it with. There is a huge choice of bricks available, and lots of brick libraries on the internet that you can peruse. Brick Match, for example, at www. brickmatch.co.uk, offers to find any brick sent to them within 24 hours, and can source a supply when a match has been made in the UK and in Europe.

Ask your architect or builder to advise on the right place to put your extension, which fits in with the requirements for planning permission. If your house is of a fairly common type in the area, you could tour your local neighbourhood to look at other extensions. If one catches your eye, the person who commissioned it may be happy to pass on the details of the architect who designed it (see Section 2 for advice on hiring an architect).

Getting the roof right is also a key consideration. If you're adding to the gable end of a house, try to follow the slope of the existing roof and match the tiles or slates.

Think about the practicalities too. Will your fuse box be able to cope with the demand from the extra sockets you're fitting in your extension, or will your

Insulation, insulation, insulation

If you're having a new kitchen or bathroom fitted and you own an older property, now is a good time to ask a builder to install some internal wall insulation. Older properties are harder to heat and adding extra insulation has the potential to cut your bills by £500 a year for an outlay of between £1,000 and £3,000, according to the Energy Saving Trust (EST).

The same applies if your builder or trader is pulling up floorboards or re-laying floors or carpets. Underfloor insulation will sit beneath the floorboards and help rooms to stay warmer in the winter. The EST estimates this will cost about £90 for materials, and could save you £50 a year, depending on how many rooms it can be installed in.

wiring need to be upgraded? Will your extension affect the amount of natural light available?

Windows will also need careful consideration – try to match the style and height of the windows used in the extension to those used on the adjacent elevation of the house. If you have an older house, bear in mind that modern casement windows will look very out of place next to original sash windows. Consider having your own windows made to measure if you can't find an off-the-shelf match.

If you're doing a loft conversion, ask your builder to check your loft insulation, as this could save you an estimated £205 a year for an outlay of £250, according to the Energy Saving Trust. A top-up is recommended if you have less than 270mm insulation.

CONSERVATORIES

Having a conservatory added to your house is a relatively painless structural process as most of the work takes place outside your home. Conservatories are mostly exempt from Building Regulations, and the duration of the job is quite short. Ask your builder to advise what design will most complement your home.

Building a conservatory is much cheaper than a brick-and-block or a timber-frame extension. However, ask your builder for a quote for the work early on – if it seems too cheap, flooring and electrics may not be included, so ensure they are to avoid ending up with just a bare shell.

Formulating a plan
BUILDERS

It's a good idea to cut out pictures of projects or finishings you've liked from newspapers, magazines and brochures so that you will have tangible images of what the final result will look like. Give your builder drawings, and brief him/her with as much detail as possible about the effect you are looking for.

For any sizeable project, run through all possible options with your architect and builder. It's important to do your homework thoroughly at this early stage and consider every possible scenario, so make sure you've addressed the following issues:

▶ Does your builder require access to your home from your neighbour's property for erecting or dismantling scaffolding?

▶ Can you get your neighbour to confirm in writing that they are happy with this arrangement?

▶ As building work is generally very noisy, agree the times with your neighbour when really loud work, such as drilling, won't cause much disruption. Doing noisy work in the evenings or over the weekend really isn't going to make you very popular.

▶ Consider what will happen if any pieces of debris fall into your neighbour's property as work goes on. To maintain good relations, it's an idea to offer to wash down any paintwork, sweep paths, pay for any windows to be cleaned, or clear up any other mess caused by your work.

CARPENTERS AND JOINERS

Discuss your plans with your carpenter/joiner for your home, and ask them to come up with a series of drawings of the work you'd like to have done, whether that's constructing floorboards, repairing or fitting doors, windows, staircases, roof trusses or partitions. Ask if they will use traditional woodworking tools, and what sort of finish or flourishes to any potentially bespoke work you should expect.

Depending on the nature of the work you're having done, your carpenter/joiner may be coming to your home in two stages for both 'first fix' and then 'second fix'. During the first phase, if your home has undergone extensive building work, they may be erecting floors and staircases, and making hatchways – a passage or an opening leading to another room – and door frames. They will return during the 'second fix' to fit architraves and skirting boards, hang doors and finish off any bespoke work you may have commissioned.

Calculate how much you will need to order in terms of materials, and whether you will need any extra time to order in or source reclaimed and rare materials.

CARPET FITTERS

Find out how much carpet or flooring material you will need to purchase. The total area of the room is technically the total surface area you'll need to carpet, but you will need more material than this to allow for fitting the carpet around awkward shapes such as fireplaces and windows. A good rule of thumb to follow here is to measure the length and width of the room in feet, then multiply the measurements to get an estimate of the surface area, adding an extra 10 per cent to allow for any extra carpet you may need.

Present this figure to sales staff, and talk to them about the size of your room(s). You could also ask for advice on how to arrange widths and lengths to reduce waste to make sure you don't over order on quantity.

It sounds obvious, but it may be a good idea to take home a sample of the carpet you're thinking of buying, and check its effect both in daylight and at night to make sure it looks good at both times of day. Remember, legally the actual carpet has to correspond to the sample. Bear in mind that the flooring you choose can make a dark room brighter, or a smaller room appear larger if you choose a light shade.

What you choose will depend on how you're using the room you're kitting out. You should ideally be looking for a flooring material that won't show wear and tear in a living room, for example, but which will still be comfortable and easy to look after. Vinyl floor tiles or linoleum might be good options for your kitchen, while it's unwise to kit out your bathroom floor in a wooden surface due to the amount of water spillage in this room. If the salesperson states that the flooring will be suitable for a particular purpose, then legally, it has to be fit for that particular purpose.

Ask your manufacturer if they recommend installing a particular type of underlay, and whether this will affect your guarantee. If you're unsure, ask your salesperson for advice.

FENCERS

Request the fencing companies you've shortlisted to send an employee to measure your property and work out how much of it will need to be fenced off, and how much this is likely to cost in materials. Make sure they also check for obstructions to installing fencing such as trees or rocks, which could hinder your project and affect the end costs. Get an exact and firm quotation. They should also check that the ground of your home or garden is level – if it slopes, this will determine how the fence is constructed.

Ask if your fence or garden wall will be exempt from planning permission – it should be, provided it is not more than 1 metre high along a boundary with a road, or 2 metres high in other places.

GARDENERS, LANDSCAPERS AND TREE SURGEONS

Some landscape gardeners will work with you to develop a concept and a plan for your garden, while others will just carry out the work you ask of them. Either way, you will need to have a good idea of what you want before you start.

Think about how you'll use the garden: for relaxing, entertaining, or for children to play in? Will you be including a vegetable patch to grow your own produce? Where does the sun fall at certain times of the day, and where are you likely to sit? Don't forget to think about practical matters such as storage, too – will you need to leave space for a shed?

Make sure you consider obvious tasks, too, such as mowing and getting rid of weeds and dead plants or trees. Could you ask your trader to replace these with flowering shrubs, for example? Buying new trees may not be a good investment; it will be a while before they add anything to the overall look.

Ask your gardener or landscaper to provide you with a detailed layout plan. Ask their advice about plants that will be suitable for your garden and its size, and find out if they are happy to provide you with a planting plan to show each

Growing your own

If you're planting a vegetable patch, ask your gardener to pinpoint the best spot in your garden, where your patch will get sun for most of the year. Make sure you're not positioning it near any existing trees or shrubs, as these will take a lot of precious water and nutrients from the soil.

Ask your gardener if you'll need to devise a windbreak in the form of a hedge or shrub to shelter your new plants. Make the most of the skill and knowledge of your gardener.

shrub in its location. Find out if your gardener will be happy to maintain your garden in the future, if applicable, or ask for tips on looking after it once they have finished their work.

When you're hiring a tree surgeon, make sure they inspect your trees beforehand to advise on any defects and decay present in the wood. Ask them about any work that can be done to increase the life-span of your trees, and get them to check that the soil in your garden will be suitable for any trees you'd like to plant. Consider getting a plan drawn up to show how new trees will look in your garden — you need to make sure you buy trees that will fit properly when they have reached their growth capacity.

GAS INSTALLERS, PLUMBERS AND ELECTRICIANS

If you're having an extensive overhaul of your home, make sure you draw up plans with your plumber as to where you'll be installing all WCs, taps and sinks. Consider where you'll be doing your laundry to fit in your washing machine, where your showers and baths may be fitted in your bathrooms if applicable, and whether there's any equipment that will require water inlets and outlets.

Talk to your plumber about whether or not you'd like to have any water-saving features installed. Devices can be fitted to WCs and taps to conserve water, and aerated shower heads are also effective. You might want to also consider buying a water-saving tank.

It might also be worth having your pipes lagged if your plumber is working with exposed pipework. Lagging hot water pipes or the cold water pipes next to them will reduce heat loss and save you money on your water bill.

For electrical improvements, draw a sketch of each room and mark where each of the electrical sockets, lights, TV aerial and phone sockets currently lie. This will help you to see how easy it may be to add a socket, or whether you will need a whole new circuit for your home. Discuss this with your electrician, and ask him/her to future-proof your home in terms of planning. For example, if you have young children now, they will grow up into teenagers with plenty of gadgets, so you may need extra sockets fitting to allow for this future demand.

If you are elderly, you might want to consider fitting more sockets in the hallway or on the landing upstairs to plug in nightlights so you can easily find your way around the house at night. Phone sockets by your bed may also be

Lights out

Energy-saving lightbulbs are fast becoming the only option available to consumers. The manufacture and import of traditional 100w incandescent lightbulbs was banned by the European Union in September 2009, although shops with these in stock won't be forced to remove them from their store. The ban will be extended to all incandescent lightbulbs by 2012.

worth investing in. Also discuss which type of energy-saving lightbulbs you'd have fitted with your electrician. These come in a wide variety of shapes and sizes now, including LED lighting and downlighting – even dimmable bulbs are available, although these are still expensive and relatively bulky.

HANDYMEN

Sit down with your trader to ensure that the jobs you would like him/her to do fit in around your builder and other tradespeople. Casual labour like this needs to be flexible.

KITCHEN AND BATHROOM FITTERS

Kitchens: Consider how you use your current kitchen, and what may be lacking. Do you eat in the kitchen, or would you like to? Is it used as a family gathering space? Are you a keen cook who needs miles of worktop space, or not into cooking, and only need to find a place for your microwave to take centre stage? Think about storage and, if you want a larder-like space in which to store food or whether cupboards will suffice.

Many kitchen suppliers can provide advice on ways to make the best ergonomic use of your kitchen, and will look into how you use your existing space and suggest improvements. Make sure that the fitters know what your exact requirements are, and what sort of materials and finish you would like to use.

When you're planning your new kitchen design, bear in mind that only a partial refit may be necessary, and ask your designer to help you with plans and drawings if you want to make alterations to your existing structure.

Make sure you also consider the following issues before you begin:

▶ Plumbing restrictions. The siting of your sink will be an issue. Sinks should go against an outside wall for drainage, and shouldn't be tucked into a corner where they can be hard to reach. Drains and outside space often determine the shape of kitchens.

▶ Are you trying to squeeze in too many appliances? This can reduce available cupboard space, and crowd out your worktop space, so take this into account when planning your design.

Make sure your fitter or manufacturer is fully aware of all your planned changes to your existing layout, and ask if you will need Building Regulations approval to carry out any of the work.

Bathrooms: Installing a new bathroom is simpler than fitting a new kitchen, and might only involve ripping out old fittings and installing new ones in their place. Consider whether you'd like to get rid of your bath in favour of a shower cubicle.

If you want to change the layout of the room, this may complicate matters. The best way to plan a new bathroom layout is to make scale drawings on squared paper, which you could ask your bathroom manufacturer to help you with. Draw individual pieces of equipment to scale, adding an area to indicate their necessary activity space, and move them around the room until you get to the best practical arrangement to suit you.

Many bathroom showrooms will offer help with bathroom planning. Tell the company or your fitter your plans, and ask if you will need to gain any Building Regulations approval for any of the work you're planning to do – if you're installing a new heating appliance or partitioning a WC from an existing bathroom, you will need to obtain this.

PAINTERS AND DECORATORS

Your painter or decorator should see the rooms they'll be painting or wallpapering before the job commences. Tell them your vision for the room(s), and check your painter/decorator will be able to provide any special paint effects you may like, such as rag rolling or marbling.

Ask your trader's advice on what the latest trends or colours are in painting or wallpaper, and work on planning a distinctive colour scheme for your home. Decide on whether your home will be able to handle any potential change – dark colours will make small rooms look even smaller, for example. If you want to go for a more minimalist look, whites and creamy shades will be flattering.

PLASTERERS

Ask your trader to come and have a look at your house so that you can discuss what you want done. Make sure they bring along a damp meter and a surface thermometer to test your walls for damp. They will be able to determine whether any holes or hairline cracks in your walls or ceilings can be replastered.

Before commissioning any work, if your home is relatively old and hasn't had much work done to it in the last 30 years, you should consider employing a surveyor or structural engineer to come and assess your home's structural soundness. If a crack in one of your walls seems to be expanding, it's a good idea to consult a structural engineer immediately.

ROOFERS

You will need to specify with your trader what materials you want to use, and how much you will need to order in terms of tiles, underlayment and shingles. If you're specifying tiles, make sure they will complement the general design of roofs in your area. If you live in a conservation area, you must check with your local authority to make sure the tiles you're choosing will be suitable. Under Section 69 of the Planning (Listed Buildings and Conservation Areas) Act 1990, you will need to gain what is known as conservation area consent from your local council to make any changes to your roof.

Ask your trader how extensive the roof repair will need to be if it is leaking. If the leak is only happening in one part of the roof, you may only need a small amount of patching work rather than replacing the whole thing.

Consider adding extra insulation in your roof or loft if your home is poorly insulated, as a quarter of a property's heat is lost through the roof. Work out how much insulation material you'll need, and what kind of material you would like to use.

Roofers

I had my roof replaced in the summer – it was a big job and everything seemed really good. However, following recent heavy rain, water has started coming in to the house. What can I do?

The roofer that carried out the work should have used reasonable skill and care in the performance of the contract. This requirement is implied in all contracts for Services under the Supply of Goods and Services Act 1982. In addition, the act provides that any materials used should be of satisfactory quality. Since you have had water coming into the house after heavy rain you can argue that either the materials were not satisfactory, or the work was not done properly. In either of these two situations, you can ask the roofer to come back and rectify the work. This should be done at no cost to you. In addition, if the water has damaged decorations or furniture internally, you are entitled to require him to put this right. This is because damage to internal decoration is foreseeable if a roofing job is not done satisfactorily.

You should contact the original roofer and inform him of the problem. He should then offer to rectify the roof and internal damage at no cost to you. If he refuses, you should seek to get another roofer to rectify the work. First, you will need to get quotes and send them to the original roofer. If he still refuses to do the work, then you should instruct one of the roofers who have given you a quote to correct the work. You will then need to recover the cost from the original roofer. If he refuses to pay, you may have to proceed to court action through the small claims court procedure (if you are claiming less than £5000 in England and Wales). (For more information on making claims, see pages 180–3)

If water is pouring through into your house, you will need to get emergency repairs done to your roof, as you have a general duty to mitigate your loss. In that scenario, you will need to get an emergency roof repair in order to safeguard your property, and then proceed as outlined above. The cost of the emergency roof repair should be recovered from the original roofer.

Green roofs – the benefits

Green roofs not only provide homes for wildlife, they will provide the following extras:

▶ Research from Ghent University in 2009 shows that having a flat green roof gives good noise insulation from noisy aircraft if you live under a flight path.

▶ If you live in a heavily built-up area, they provide a precious sighting of green space.

▶ They soak up rain and delay run-off from the roof.

▶ The industry association Green Roofs for Healthy Cities has found that green roofs can lengthen the lifespan of a roof membrane by two to three times, as it shields it from UV radiation.

Insulation material comes in three main types: quilts, which are man-made from glass or rock fibre, with mineral wool being the UK's most common form of loft-insulation quilt; blown insulation, which is blown loosely into specific areas, and is made from newspapers; and boards, which are made from expanded polystyrene. The Energy Saving Trust (EST) recommends that you use a minimum depth of 270mm in your roof, but in theory, the deeper your insulation is, the better, as the less heat you'll lose.

You might also want to consider installing a green roof system on your roof. Green roofs are becoming increasingly popular in heavily built-up areas, as they are excellent for reducing noise pollution, along with the numerous other benefits they offer – see box above. This will comprise a series of waterproofing and drainage layers which will be covered in plants. You can buy blankets of vegetation that can be easily rolled out. Ask your roofer if your roof is pitched at less than 30 degrees, and how much weight your roof should be able to take to accommodate the soil and plants on top.

WINDOW FITTERS

Make sure the salesperson who visits your home to take your order is fully aware of your budget, and is happy to let you choose the type of windows you would like to be fitted. Salespeople have courted bad press in recent years for their tendency to steer consumers towards their company's most expensive products, without taking into account the types of windows that would actually complement your home. Don't be pushed into choosing something you don't feel will be right. Remember that the Consumer Protection from Unfair Trading Regulations 2007 contains prohibitions against misleading and aggressive practices. So if you feel that means of harassment, coercion or undue influence were used, contact your local Trading Standards.

Consider extras, such as security features and window handles. If you live in an area with serious noise pollution, getting double glazed windows as soon as possible will greatly reduce any outside noise. UPVC windows generally provide the best insulation for double glazing, although these may not be in keeping with the style of your home if you own an older property. Under Section 69 of the Planning (Listed Buildings and Conservation Areas) Act 1990, you'll need to gain permission from your local council to install UPVC windows if your home is listed or lies within a conservation area.

If you live in a conservation area, you must always check the type of window you would like to have fitted with your local authority to make sure it's in line with their requirements.

Itemising payment

The costs for various jobs by traders will fluctuate widely according to the area you live in, the nature of the work and the skill of your contractor. In general, never pay the full quoted cost for your work upfront. This is your bargaining tool in case anything needs fixing when the work is completed, and stops your trader disappearing with your money.

Bear in mind that if your trader is charging a daily rate, it's possible that they won't be in a hurry to complete the job, so push for a full, comprehensive quote. If they want to charge by the day or hour, make sure you agree on a rate and the hours you want them to work, preferably putting this in writing.

Establish whether your quotation includes material, parts and labour costs. Traders often prefer to order their own materials and then charge the client at the end of the job. This can be beneficial, as they can buy up materials at trade prices – although there is nothing to prevent them making a profit on the transaction.

When you're putting down a deposit or making interim payments, make sure you get signed receipts from the trader and keep them in a safe place. Find out if the trader has insurance to cover deposits should they go bust – some trade associations require members to take this out.

If you are buying the materials yourself, make sure you have ordered everything on the builder's shopping list, or the job could be held up.

Establish whether your initial quotation includes VAT. Your contractor must be VAT registered to charge it to your bill, and when sizeable sums are involved, it pays to check the registration with your local VAT office. Unscrupulous and unregistered firms have been known to add VAT to bills as an illegal way of making more profit out of unsuspecting and gullible clients.

If relevant, your contract could include an itemised schedule of works describing the work to be carried out, and the price paid for each item of work.

If it is not possible to get an exact and firm quote, ask your trader to provide you with a rough estimate of total costs, and try to get this in writing to ensure they will stick to it. Ask them to notify you immediately about any problems or issues that could affect the cost throughout the work. Also make it a requirement that any changes to the specification are to be confirmed in writing, before any additional works go ahead. Remember that you are only liable for work you have authorised.

Never be tempted to go for a lower price that's quoted for cash. If things go wrong, you will need receipts and invoices, along with other relevant information as proof of any costs you have incurred, things you are unlikely to get from a cash-in-hand trader.

PLAN YOUR PAYMENTS

Planning your payments is crucial if you're borrowing money for the work, or dipping into your savings, as you shouldn't be paying the full cost of the work upfront. For example, if the total project costs £30,000, you may need:

▶ £5,000 for materials at the start of the work.
▶ £10,000 after six weeks.
▶ Another £10,000 12 weeks later.
▶ The final £5,000 when the work is finished.

Be clever with your cash. Keeping your money in a savings account or not paying the interest on the borrowed amount, could save you hundreds of pounds to put towards extras later on.

LET YOUR CREDIT CARD TAKE THE STRAIN

If you have the chance to put down any money on a credit card to pay for your home improvements, take it. As long as the value of the contract is between £100 and £30,000, and you've paid using your credit card (even just the deposit), you will be covered for any breaches of contract or misrepresentation or if your trader goes bust under Section 75 of the Consumer Credit Act 1974, and your credit card provider will have to stump up the cash if you're out of pocket. This protection doesn't apply to payments made on debit cards.

However, you might also have a chance of getting something back if you've paid for any work on a Visa debit card. You could get some of the cash returned using the Visa Debit Chargeback system. Call your bank to find out if you're covered under this.

BUILDERS

Building work is often paid for in stages. If this is the case with your work, you should have stipulated in your original contract the frequency and conditions of interim payments, such as the amount of work that must be completed before payment is due and the amount of retention money, usually 5 per cent, which is not paid until any defective work is put right.

Make sure your contract includes an itemised schedule of works describing the work to be carried out, and the price paid for each item of work.

CARPENTERS AND JOINERS

To fit an internal or external door, expect to pay between £265 and £855, depending on the quality of the work and the materials used, which may vary enormously. To build and fit cupboards should cost you £900 and upwards.

CARPET FITTERS

Prices for fitting a carpet are worked out on a square metre basis. Check that the price of the carpet and any underlay and other fittings, such as door plates, are itemised separately. Doors may need to be removed and shaved to fit, so check if this is also included in the price. If there is any furniture in the room, either you or the fitter will have to move it in advance of the carpet being laid. Check who is to do this – and if it's the fitter, will you be charged? You will be expected to pay as soon as the job has been finished to your satisfaction.

FENCERS

Your quote will vary depending on what sort of fencing you are erecting and should be broken down into materials and time. Check on whether or not the fencer charges VAT.

GAS INSTALLERS, PLUMBERS AND ELECTRICIANS

Most electricians, gas installers and plumbers and many other contractors and traders charge by the hour for their time, but the cost of some jobs can be pinned down at an early stage.

Check what the call-out fee is before you hire, and ask how much materials will add on to the price to get an estimate of the overall cost. Find out if VAT is included in the price, or if this will be added to your bill.

HANDYMEN

Similarly, quotes will most likely be based on an hourly charge. Ensure you establish this in advance of any work getting underway and, if possible, find out how long your handyperson thinks the job will take. Materials will no doubt be extra, which you may or may not prefer to source for yourself.

KITCHEN AND BATHROOM FITTERS

To install a new 3 x 4m kitchen will cost on average £8,840. A new bathroom is lower in price to fit, coming in at between £1,900 and £2,050 on average. If installation costs are included in your package, don't pay the full amount upfront, and hold back at least 20 per cent of the fee until the job is finished. This should ensure that any items missing or extra work that needs to be done will be dealt with before you pay the total amount.

PAINTERS AND DECORATORS

To paint a 4 x 4m room with two coats of paint should cost in the region of £345. Painting the exterior of a three-bedroom house will cost significantly more, ranging from £2,580 to £3,580.

PLASTERERS

It should cost £500 for a trader to plaster a 4 x 4m room, applying one coat of lightweight bonding plaster. To remove plaster and re-plaster the same sized room will cost £970, and £1,430 on average if the plasterer replaces and repaints your skirting boards.

ROOFERS

Re-covering a standard gable-ended roof with plain tiles will cost upwards of £3,460. Repairing a roof with localised replacement or cracked or slipped tiles will be on average £515. A large job, requiring more than 10–20 per cent of your tiles to be replaced, is likely to require scaffolding. Ask your roofer how much this could add to the overall cost, and request an estimate upfront so there are no nasty surprises in store at the end of the job when you receive your bill.

WINDOW FITTERS

Make sure you have received all quotations in writing beforehand, but don't expect to pay more than £630 to fit a typical casement window of 1.2 x 1.2m. To install double glazing for seven windows in a two-storey home will cost between £4,429 and £7,740. Check if you will need to pay the fitters anything extra on the day.

Timescales and schedules

The amount of time any improvement work will take will depend on the nature of the job you've commissioned, the state of your property or the state of your contractor's diary – they may ask to return after doing the first phase of work at a later date if they are particularly busy. However, the time taken for some jobs can be estimated, as we've noted below.

It's important to stipulate specific timeframes in your contract, and the order in which you'd like the work to be done. Your builder may have a standard contract template, in which such information can be set out. Or if you've hired an architect or a surveyor, they will almost certainly use a standard template as supplied by the Royal Institute of British Architects (RIBA) or the Royal Institute of Chartered Surveyors (RICS) . If not, you could draw one up yourself.

The Federation of Master Builders (FMB) provides a free and easy to understand 'Plain English' contract, which you can use with any builder, even those who aren't FMB members. You can download one online at their website, www.fmb.org.uk.

If you're commissioning major improvement works, include a clause in your contract outlining the exact number of days' absence that you will tolerate before damages are incurred. This will apply if a contractor is regularly failing to

The schedule of works

If you are planning a particularly big project, draw up a schedule of works, a document that details an overview of the entire job. This will break down the work into simple stages, detailing payment and completion schedules for each phase. It should essentially be a summary of the specification with additional information. Try to draw this up on a single sheet of A4 to keep it simple. A typical example might be:

Weeks 1–2: Site preparation, plumbing installation
Week 3: Bathroom completed, first payment due
Week 4: Preliminary work on kitchen begins

This way, if you get to the end of week 4 and the bathroom isn't finished but the builder or trader is still asking for payment, you have an at-a-glance list with which to make a judgement.

appear on site. This clause should provide a fixed level of damages, known as liquidated damages, per week, by way of compensation.

If you're having a number of jobs completed at the same time as part of a big project, then timescales are absolutely crucial as time delays cost money. In any case, you risk setting off a 'domino effect' of setbacks, which will affect every trader working on your project. If you're managing the project yourself, you must make sure you know what needs to be done and in what order.

BUILDERS

Before your builder arrives, bear in mind that building work is very unpredictable. Even if it goes well, it will be a stressful experience. There are often too many variables in play for work to proceed as you've planned, so it's a good idea to make a detailed plan of action with your builder.

Building an extension

The sequence of events for building an extension should go in the following order:

▶ The site is cleared, and the area where the foundations will lie is marked out.

▶ Foundations digging commences. Extensions require deep foundations and extra drainage, including allowing for extra water to come off the roof. A lot of mud will need to be dug up and transported out of the garden.

▶ The walls will go up. Bear in mind that block or brick walls are labour-intensive to construct, but in a timber-frame construction, the inner walls will appear as if by magic.

▶ Upper-floor joists are built in.

▶ The roof is added.

▶ Wiring, plumbing and heating are put in place.

▶ Plastering is carried out – the last of the really messy jobs.

▶ Skirtings and decorating are completed. You could consider taking this task on yourself to save money and to start taking possession of the project as soon as possible. This whole process should take from eight to twelve months from planning to construction. It can take much longer, however, if all does not go according to plan.

Building a conservatory

Building a conservatory should take approximately six weeks. Plan the project in the following order:

▶ The site is cleared and excavated. This means levelling off the ground and repositioning downpipes.

▶ Foundations are laid and a 'dwarf' wall installed to carry the walls of the conservatory.

▶ The base is put down. Ask your builder to follow closely the specific instructions that come with this from the manufacturer.

▶ The structure is erected. This is usually made of modular steel, aluminium, PVC or timber.

▶ The roof and side panels are glazed.

▶ The electrical supply is connected, wall lights are fitted and wired up, the ceiling fan connected and the electrical supply connected to the mains. The heating radiators are connected up.

▶ Finally, plastering takes place, and finishes such as painting, varnishing woodwork and floor treatments are applied. Plastering will conceal any electrical cables or plumbing work, although many people choose to leave the existing wall finish as bare brick, render, stucco or pebbledash.

Break down the job into itemised phases with an agreed timescale. Reputable contractors should produce a programme of events with an overall time or completion date stated. Depending on the nature of the job, you could ask when critical stages, such as breaking through into your home from an extension, will be carried out.

CARPENTERS AND JOINERS

To fit an internal or external door should take two to three hours, although fitting a door may take longer if the frame is out of shape, as the door will have to be trimmed to fit. External doors may take longer if they need to be fitted with more locks. Fitted cupboards will take two days to build, and one to two days to fit. They are put together in a workshop by a joiner, and then assembled on site.

CARPET FITTERS

One of the last jobs to be done, you need to ensure that the floors are scrupulously clean before the carpets are laid. If doors need fitting, consider doing this after the carpets have been laid to avoid unnecessary hanging and re-hanging.

FENCERS

This can be fitted into your schedule at any time since it is unlikely to impede on work within the house. You will most probably want to ensure the fences are in place before any gardeners or landscapers appear on the scene. They will give them a clear indication as to where the boundaries fall and what may need disguising or growing plants up or along.

GARDENERS, LANDSCAPERS AND TREE SURGEONS

If your building project is to be carried over a few seasons, plan for your gardening or landscaping to be done in the spring or autumn. Any newly bought plants will then have time to settle before the heat of summer or frosty winters, which will give them a greater chance of survival. It is also good use of time to dig over soil in the cooler months.

GAS INSTALLERS, PLUMBERS AND ELECTRICIANS

The following guide times should give you an approximate estimate of how long the most common heating and plumbing jobs should take:
▶ Conducting a safety gas check: 1 hour
▶ Replacing a dishwasher: 1 hour
▶ Installing an outside tap or gas hob: 2 hours
▶ Replacing a radiator: 2 hours
▶ Replacing a WC: 3–4 hours
▶ Fitting a bedroom/bathroom sink: 5–6 hours
▶ Installing a boiler: 1 day

Planning a timeframe for electrical work may be more difficult as every property's wiring is different. Electrical work often takes place in two stages – 'first fix', laying the initial wiring, replacing a fuse box or re-wiring, and then moving on to the 'second fix', which is fitting sockets after plastering or decorating. The entire job may take a week, but could be split into, for example, three days in one week to do the 'first fix' and then another two days later on to finish the 'second fix'.

HANDYMEN

Schedule any handymen you are employing to suit the other tradespeople as these smaller tasks can be built in around the more major electrical, plumbing, flooring and tiling jobs.

KITCHEN AND BATHROOM FITTERS

A new kitchen should take between four to five days on average to fit, while a bathroom takes three to five days. If you want a built-in shower to be installed in your new bathroom, this will add another two to three days on top.

Having any sort of work done in the home is disruptive, especially in two of your property's most important rooms. Ask how long exactly you will be left without your bathroom or kitchen. The inconvenience of living without these facilities is not to be taken lightly. If you have children, they may be better off

Bespoke fittings

If you are having things specially made for your home, extra care may be necessary. You should allow enough time for the manufacture and arrival of specially crafted goods, especially if they are being flown in from abroad. Consider the bigger picture too. For example, non-standard kitchen units may be too big to fit in with your other units, worktops, dishwashers or cookers. Measure everything beforehand, or arrange to have an onsite survey before placing an order.

staying with friends or relatives unless there will be a guaranteed, seamless transition from the old to the new facilities in a single day, which is very unlikely. Bear in mind that such an easy transition is more often promised than it is achieved.

Ask your fitter to provide a clear plan of action, and try to ensure it is stuck to. Make sure they brief you on what to expect every day so that disruption is minimised for you, and make sure they have planned the installation well in advance. It may be worth asking for a day-by-day forward plan before work commences.

The same issues apply to bathroom fitting. It's another room you really can't afford to be without for long. Critical to your quality of life will be the speed and efficiency of the changeover from old to new basic facilities, so make sure that you know exactly how long this will take, and ask your fitters to draw up a detailed timeplan.

Bear in mind that before any work begins, ordering in appliances such as fridges, washing machines and cookers can take weeks. The same applies to bathroom furniture and tiles, so make sure everything you need for the job will be available when you want it, and not several weeks later. A finished bathroom waiting for some taps to arrive from Italy is not a finished bathroom, but a major and costly inconvenience.

PAINTERS AND DECORATORS

To paint a 4 x 4m room with two coats of paint should take one painter a day. This time will include painting the ceiling and painting gloss on the skirting boards and architraves around the door. Decorators will need to leave time for the paint to dry between applying each coat.

Painting the outside of a three-bedroom house may take two painters one week. To gloss paint fascias and soffits (the flat board under the eaves and fascia) properly, decorators should remove guttering and replace it afterwards.

PLASTERERS

It should take half a day to a day to plaster a 4 x 4m room before decoration, applying one coat of lightweight bonding plaster. The time taken to remove plaster and replaster a 4 x 4m room, including replacing and painting new skirting boards, should be two to three days. Add extra time to these estimates if you are having any decoration done. You'll need a gap of several days while the plaster dries out before you get the decorators in.

ROOFERS

Re-covering a standard gable-ended roof with plain tiles should take on average three days. Repairing a roof with localised replacement of cracked or slipped tiles will take a day if the firm provides you with two workers.

If you own a thatched roof, bear in mind that this incredibly labour-intensive job will probably take a few weeks to complete.

WINDOW FITTERS

Replacing a typical casement window which measures roughly 1.2 x 1.2m should take two to three hours per window. Replacing sash windows takes significantly longer, and you should expect to work around a timeframe of three to four days if, for example, you are installing new double glazing for seven windows in a two-storey home.

What to do before the job starts

Because of the nature of home improvements, any work you are going to have done is likely to be extremely disruptive. Prepare as much as you can in advance for the chaos that will ensue to ensure the work goes as smoothly as possible, and pack away any valuables in a safe place.

Let your neighbours know if you're having any work done, as they could be inconvenienced by the noise and potential mess from the work. Check that piles of sand won't be trodden into anyone's lawn, for example.

IN THE HOME

Before your carpet or flooring is fitted, make sure the floor underneath is dry, clean and smooth, unless you already have an existing carpet or flooring, and you've arranged that your fitters will be taking it up. Move all furniture into another area, and vacuum the room thoroughly before the fitters arrive.

Ask the installer if you will need to take the carpet/flooring up yourself beforehand, or if they will provide this service for you – if it's the firm you've bought your carpets from is doing the fitting, you may have to pay extra for this.

If you're having any type of flooring fitted in your kitchen, you will need to remove any free-standing appliances, and turn off the water and gas. In your bathroom, you should remove the WC and sink to fit flooring underneath, as this will prevent water going into the gap. You should call a plumber in to do this.

Before your builder arrives on site, move everything out of the affected area that you don't want to be damaged, leaving behind only things that are destined for the skip. If there is major work to be done, such as knocking down internal walls or stripping out a kitchen or bathroom, most people clear everything out down to the carpets or the lino, but it may be worthwhile going even further.

Carpets may need to come up and go to the tip, and if there is floor sanding to be done, then the carpet grip around the edge of the room needs to be levered up with a crowbar. Doing any light stripping-out work yourself will save your builder charging for half a day of his skilled time, and the work will help you to adjust to your new living conditions.

If you decide to do any preliminary demolition work yourself, make sure you do a good job of it. Don't leave lots of mess lying around for the builders to clear up – no one likes finishing someone else's job. Be sure to tell your builder that you're going to do it yourself, or he'll bill it into his costs anyway.

Dealing with builders

You have every right to set out the terms under which builders will work in your home. You can't expect them to change into carpet slippers every time they cross the threshold, but you should make your ground rules clear from the start. Discuss with your builder well in advance what working space, storage and access are needed to do the job.

Building work is nearly always messy, so make sure you protect your home from the worst by taking the follow precautions:

▶ Buy plastic sheeting and tape to seal off unaffected areas. Treat the other side of it like a contaminated zone, refusing to allow debris to pass through, or you will soon be enveloped by seeping dust.

▶ You can also put tape around doors and block up the gap at the bottom with rolled-up newspaper or rags. Make sure you pack away all breakable items.

▶ Plan the builders' best access route into or through your house. Remove as much furniture from this path as possible, and ask your builder to put down heavy-duty plastic runners, so that wet or muddy boots don't mark your floor coverings through the plastic.

▶ You may also want to tape protective packing material to any door frames through which tools and materials will have to pass.

▶ Insist that internal doors are kept shut whenever possible to prevent dust spreading right through the house, and use dust sheets.

▶ Ask your builders to leave their muddy shoes on the other side of the plastic if they have to trek into your area for any reason.

Make sure that deliveries to the site won't cause an obstruction, especially if they're being left in the road. You need permission from your local authority highways department to do this, also to park a skip in the road. Establish in advance who will be responsible for obtaining the necessary permits – you or your builder. You can obtain one by contacting your local authority's highways department.

If you're having any scaffolding erected outside for building an extension, now may be the time to invest in some extra security locks for your upstairs windows, because walking into your bedroom will become as easy a job for intruders as climbing up a ladder from the street.

Consider where you're going to store the materials for the project, and make sure you have enough space available. These principles should also apply to any improvement works you've commissioned.

Carefully pack away all your appliances, crockery and cutlery in boxes to be stored in a safe place. Turn off the electricity in this room at the mains and the water supply, then disconnect all appliances and move them into another room. Your fitter may be happy to provide this service for you, albeit at extra cost, so check before moving any heavy objects.

If you own any gas appliances, these need to be disconnected by a Gas Safe registered professional.

IN THE GARDEN

Clear the area where work will take place of any garden paraphernalia, such as statues, benches or children's toys.

If you are laying the ground for a new vegetable patch, you should clear the site of weeds beforehand, as well as removing any rubbish or sizeable stones.

Ask your gardener/landscaper/tree surgeon where they would like to sit when taking a break. You may prefer to set up an old table and chairs in the garage or garden shed for their use if you're not prepared to let them into your kitchen.

You should notify your neighbours if you're having any work done. This includes tree felling. Although your tree surgeon will have planned and measured the direction the tree will fall in when it's cut down, greatly reducing the risk of damage to your neighbours' property, the noise created by the work will be substantial.

RUNNING THE PROJECT

There's an awful lot that can go wrong when it comes to home improvement works. No job ever goes according to plan. Worst-case scenarios are discovering after work has started that the entire house needs underpinning, or that the remains of a Roman temple are lurking beneath the spot where you were going to lay your patio.

But if you've planned effectively beforehand, and you've taken the appropriate precautions to protect the areas of your home that aren't having a facelift, the odds of hitting disaster could be seriously diminished. If you've done your homework thoroughly, you should find the job will be fairly straightforward and stay within expected parameters.

Have a contingency plan for all eventualities, and tick off the following as you go along:

▸ Have you cleared a good working space for your traders?
▸ Do you need to get a parking permit for your trader's van?
▸ Will you need to hire a skip?
▸ Have you told your neighbours about the work?
▸ Have you agreed who will obtain Building Regulations approval?

As work goes on, you should be meticulous about clearing the decks as far as is possible at the end of each day or session, to avoid turning your whole home

Watch out for unexpected damage

You must take care that your vulnerable new fittings aren't damaged by the continuing work around them. If you're having lots of work done, you may have traders rushing through your home constantly, and just a tiny knock will be enough to cause serious damage to delicate home fixtures. Consider putting masking tape around fixtures to prevent scratches, or better still, a rag that is secured so that handles of new cupboards and doors are still usable, but given padded protection.

into a building site. Ask for paths and other areas to be swept at the end of each working day to minimise the transfer of materials into your house.

Keeping records

It's a good idea to keep a log of how the work is going, as a simple project diary – recording the key events of each day can prove invaluable later on if disputes arise. Note down when materials arrive, when the building control officer visited,

---

What to do if you uncover asbestos

If you're having work done on an older property, you risk finding asbestos. The material has been known for its fire-retardant properties since the time of the ancient Greeks, but in the 1970s, it was discovered to cause a degenerative lung disease called mesothelioma and lung cancer.

It's not uncommon to find it in domestic conversions – large quantities of it were used to build homes in the 1950s, 1960s and early 1970s. If your home was built during this period, contact your local council and ask them if your home is likely to contain asbestos. Asbestos isn't easy to recognise, and often the only way to be sure that you've found it is to send it to a laboratory to be tested, but it could have been used in any of the following:

▶ Eaves, gutters and rainwater pipes
▶ Floor tiles
▶ Bath panels
▶ Wall, ceiling and door linings
▶ Central heating flues
▶ Asbestos packing between floors and in partition walls
▶ Insulation panels in storage heaters.

You should record its existence if you find it for the benefit of future occupants of your home, informing your trader of its presence in your home, and leave it undisturbed, unless it is broken or chipped, in which case it should be removed as soon as possible. You can find a licensed asbestos removal company in your area by searching the Asbestos Removal Contractors Association's (ARCA) online directory at www.arca.org.uk.

and when, for example, the electrician admitted responsibility for dropping his pliers in the bath and chipping the enamel. Take pictures if possible. You should also mark down in the log any changes to the specification that may have been agreed.

The main advantage of keeping a record is that if, at the end of the month, the builder is falling behind but still wants their full monthly instalment and is arguing that any delays incurred were unavoidable due to rain, or the plumber wants to charge you for half a day's work here or there, you will have a tangible record to go on.

Before you allow work to begin, check that all the parts for your new fittings are undamaged. Raise any concerns you might have with your fitter when they come up, rather than waiting until the end when it might be too late to fix some issues.

Keep a record of the work that's been done, and whether you've needed to make any changes to the specification – if you've had to use different tiles than the ones you originally wanted, this could spoil your enjoyment of the finished product. In the bathroom or kitchen, difficulties with fitting your preferred plumbing product may have reshaped your rooms in ways you hadn't intended. If your fitters/plumbers argue that your original plan can only be implemented if they charge extra, you might want to consider compromising. Be reasonable.

Checking the work

Most traders hate to be monitored while they work, so it's probably best to check all work at the end of each day. If you're not in during the day, leave phone numbers with your trader to make sure they can contact you if there are any problems.

For smaller jobs, it is best to be present throughout in case any snap decisions need to be made, and so you can let your trader in and out of your home easily.

If you've hired a tree surgeon, you will definitely need to be there on the day to make any snap decisions in case any trees need to be cut down if they are diseased, for example, or in the event of other problems arising. With all gardening work in general, it's important to make sure you are there so that you get the result you want, as the plans you've given to your gardeners may need to be altered and reworked. For example, the spot you've chosen for your vegetable patch may need to be moved if your gardener considers it to be too exposed, so you may need to have a quick rethink on the design.

Keep all paperwork on your project in a safe place, including copies of your contract, cost estimates and any receipts you may have accumulated. It may be worth setting up a file and dividing all the paperwork – receipts, quotations, contracts, and so on – into easy-to-find sections. It is also worth keeping a record of the work as it progresses, and possibly taking photographs as the job goes along if it is particularly extensive. Before and after shots will be helpful in the event of a future dispute.

KEEP AN EYE ON PROGRESS

If you are supervising the project yourself, it's not a great idea to get too involved in the day-to-day running of the work. You'll only get in the way and annoy your workmen, who may object to being watched while they work. Your main priority should be to ensure that the job is carried out according to the specification and the contract. Step in immediately if you see something that is in obvious breach of the contract, but raise the issue carefully rather than losing your temper.

Check how the work is going each evening, and if you find anything amiss, you can either telephone the contractor there and then, or leave written instructions to be read the next morning.

On long-running projects, it's an idea to suggest a regular weekly meeting to discuss how it's coming along with your builder, and iron out any problems. If you're not at home during the day, leave details with your builder of where you can be contacted if necessary.

Wear loose and comfortable old clothes whenever you're making checks on the work. Watch out for nails sticking out of pieces of wood such as upturned floorboards – most shoes offer no protection against injury from protruding pieces of metal.

It's your builder's responsibility to make sure all his/her contractors on site are familiar with health and safety information, and to ensure that all equipment is safe to use. If you see anything that goes against this – a subcontractor not being supplied with a protective breathing mask when laying roof insulation,

Keep a snagging list

Make what is known as a snagging list as you go around the site, noting any defects or deviations from your specification, or things that you're not happy with, such as missing fittings or poor finishes.

Raise any problems tactfully with your builder. They understand about snagging lists, and won't be offended or insulted to be told of things that will need to be redone as long as you handle it properly, ideally at a prearranged snagging meeting on site.

A snagging list is basically an inventory of all faults and defects you may come across after the work has been carried out. You should spend at least a couple of hours when the work is completed noting down faults for the list, checking each part of your home that's undergone work. Details of the following should be noted on every defect found:

▶ A description of the fault.
▶ The name of the person responsible.
▶ A target date for fixing the defect.

Once you've jotted down all visible defects, type up the snagging list and give it to your builder, keeping a copy for your own records. Make sure you get any assurances to redo unsatisfactory work in writing.

You can purchase a snagging guide from www.snagging.org.

for example – raise the matter with your builder and insist that he/she complies with the guidelines.

Check where materials are being stored at the end of each day – is it in a safe place, or left out as an open invitation for intruders to come and pillage your garden? Also make sure, if you're using scaffolding, that your trader makes access to it difficult by removing ladders or fixing a scaffold board over the rungs of the ladder to deter intruders.

Onsite tidiness is a serious health and safety issue that you will need to monitor regularly, as rubble and discarded tools can present a serious hazard. Time spent clearing up will increase efficiency as workers will be able to move about the site more easily, and see what needs to be done and what has already been accomplished. The same applies if you're having any gardening work done – keep the area tidy and free of any potential hazards.

Delays and rising costs

It is common for any improvement work you have done to run over the timescale you've set. Poor weather could set back any building or gardening project for days, for example. Keep daily records of the work that's been done, and ask your trader to report delays to you each day. If you feel you're being taken advantage of, you can impose penalties accordingly (if you have set out an appropriate clause detailing this in your contract – see pages 30–1).

If the project isn't turning out as you'd envisaged, that's a different matter. Talk to your trader or project manager immediately. You may find that minor defects are being tolerated in the work to make sure the job runs smoothly, and that everything is being properly noted down in a snagging list by your trader or project manager, and will be rectified before the project is completed. Make sure you establish whether or not this is the case. Trying to resolve things in a conversation is preferable to writing a formal letter in the first instance.

But you shouldn't tolerate any of the following in any work you commission:

▶ Any materials that have been left out and are unsafe.
▶ Excessive levels of dirt or untidiness.
▶ Gaps between joinery, such as skirting and architraves.
▶ Poor finishes.
▶ Noisy plumbing.
▶ Wobbly appliances.
▶ Wonky worktops.
▶ Bathroom or kitchen furniture that isn't level.
▶ Fixtures that are poorly secured – but first check that this will be rectified before the job is finished.

Using a specialist project manager

If you've employed an architect or a surveyor (see Section 2) to supervise your project, make sure he/she visits the site at regular intervals, and will handle all the necessary communication with the contractors. This shouldn't prevent you from taking an interest in how the work is progressing, but remember that you should pass any comments or complaints you might have to your project manager rather than making them directly to the contractors.

▶ Untidy gardening work.

▶ The lack of a good sub-base if you have had a new drive paved.

If you are genuinely dissatisfied with any of the above and your trader/project manager refuses to act, you should invoke the terms of your contract and withhold payment for that portion of the work. Even if there is nothing in your contract about poor workmanship, or you don't have a contract, you can still withhold a sum equivalent to the cost of remedial work. Do pay for the portion of work you are satisfied with, however.

WITHHOLDING FULL PAYMENT

Withholding full payment because you're dissatisfied with *one* aspect of the job is unreasonable – you should pay for all the work that has been completed to your satisfaction. Calculating what sum to withhold from your trader is tricky. It's a good idea to get an opinion about the likely cost of the remedial work from a surveyor (see Section 2), who will also be able to act as an expert if required. Then give your trader the chance to complete the job properly. If the work was done so poorly that you've lost all faith in their ability, you could use the withheld sum to employ another trader.

KEEPING CALM

Confrontation produces adrenaline, which can lead to physical hostility, so take precautions against getting carried away by the moment. Before confronting anyone about work you're not happy with, imagine yourself dealing with your trader confidently. Have a plan of action so you know what you're going to discuss with them, and try not to threaten the trader or make sarcastic remarks. It might help to say that you've taken further advice and that you want to resolve the matter amicably. Try to avoid falling out with your trader.

ESCALATING COSTS

You should have established a price with your contractor before any work commenced, but if you were only given a rough estimate and you are receiving far more sizeable bills than you were expecting for labour, under the Supply of Goods and Services Act (1982), the trader can only charge a 'reasonable amount' for the work.

To find out what a reasonable price is for the work, contact the relevant trade association to ask for a guide to charges. You could also ask several other traders what they would have charged for the same job. You should then give the trader a cheque for what you believe to be a reasonable amount, saying that this is in full and final settlement. If the trader cashes your cheque, they will be deemed to have accepted your offer. If the trader doesn't accept your offer, they will have to take you to court to retrieve the money.

Hopefully, you will have budgeted for unforeseen expenses in material costs, for example, when setting aside a budget for your project. But if a problem occurs in your project that you feel your trader should have spotted beforehand that raises costs substantially – if, for example, your whole home is riddled with dry rot – ask your trader how they intend to rectify the situation, and whether they will shoulder or share the costs with you.

POOR QUALITY WORKMANSHIP

Any work you commission should be done in a workmanlike manner, using materials of satisfactory quality. The quality of workmanship can be argued about indefinitely, but if it's good quality, it shouldn't give rise to debate. A serious trader will want to know exactly what you mean when you criticise their work on these grounds.

HALF-FINISHED PROJECTS?

If your trader goes bust through no fault of their own, or is unable to complete the work owing to ill health or accidents, if you've taken out an insurance backed guarantee (IBG, see page 33), you may be covered for the completion of unfinished work if the contractor concerned is a member of a trade association. The Building Guarantee Scheme (BGS) offered by the Construction Employers Federation (CEF) will cover unfinished work up to the value of £15,000, and also provides a six-month defects liability period, followed by a two-year cover period for structural defects.

Under the conditions of a Homepro IBG, your policy will provide cash for an approved contractor under the conditions of your IBG to remedy the work if your contractor ceases to trade during the policy's guarantee period, which can be anything up to ten years. The policy will also return your deposit, which is covered for a maximum of 90 days from when you had a receipt from your trader for the money. Deposit protection stops, however, when work starts on site.

But if your trader's business folds, unless you have a guarantee in place, or have paid a deposit by credit card, you'll have little hope of getting your money back and may have to take the loss.

You can check if your trader's business has gone bankrupt or into administration for free if it is listed as a limited company at Companies House (www.companieshouse.gov.uk). If the business has gone into administration, a process during which a company calls in accountants to help to save its business, there's nothing to really stop your job being completed by your existing trader.

Keep in touch with your trader, and take down their administrator's contact details in case you need to make a claim in the future. There is the risk, however, that the company will become insolvent, when you will need to apply to be added to a list of creditors.

UNPAID BILLS

If unpaid subcontractors or suppliers are clamouring for payment, don't be tempted to pay them off yourself, as your contract should state that their wages or material costs are the responsibility of the main contractor, who will probably owe you money too because he/she is in breach of contract. Even if there is nothing along these lines in the contract, if you only agreed to pay the trader for the work done, and certain responsibilites have been subcontracted to others, then the main trader is responsible for paying them. Your position will be different, however, if you have agreed to pay the subcontractors directly.

You may be able to keep any tools or materials that have been left onsite to sell to cover your costs, provided these belong to your trader and haven't been hired. However, often subcontractors will have sensed the impending financial disaster – not being paid is a pretty good indicator of this – and they may have already removed any tools belonging to the trader that aren't nailed down.

GETTING YOUR MONEY BACK

If you have paid for your work on your credit card, then your card issuer is jointly and severally liable for any breaches of contract or misrepresentations against your trader.

Putting down any amount of cash ranging from between £100 and £30,000 on a credit card gives you the chance to invoke Section 75 of the Consumer Credit Act to claim back your deposit and any other expenses. You don't even need to have paid for all the work on your card – even a small deposit will make the card company liable, and then you will have the cash to pay someone else to complete the work.

Ring your credit card company and tell them you want to make a Section 75 claim. Request a claim form, and state on the form this section of the act again. You might also have a chance of getting something back if you've paid for any work on a Visa debit card. You could get some of the cash returned using the Visa Debit Chargeback system. Call your bank to find out if you're covered under this.

If you paid for the work using another type of debit card, you may not have any luck, but it's still worth ringing your bank to see if you're covered in any way.

DESIGN CHANGES

It's easy to lose perspective in the middle of a building programme. Days and even weeks seem to merge into one another and little seems to have been achieved, apart from potential damage to your house.

Keep an eye on what's happening during the laying of foundations and the building of walls and supporting piers, if applicable, at the beginning of the work. It's a good idea to monitor the basic layout of new walls as they are marked out, even at the very early bricklaying stage. It's not unusual for designs to change even at this stage.

If something isn't turning out as you'd imagined, it may still be possible to alter the final layout. Sometimes partitions are moved when it becomes clear that the dimensions are impracticable. For example, en suite bathrooms are often scaled down into shower rooms when it becomes clear that there either won't be enough space for the bath or the bed in the next room.

If you've witnessed any setbacks that have caused delays – poor weather conditions, late arrival of supplies or other unforeseen problems – it's easy to sympathise with the builder and let deadlines slide. But it's crucial to remain firm, negotiate any alterations to the deadline formally, and then to make a note of the new arrangements in writing in your log book. Recording weather conditions daily will also be useful. You could even get confirmation of this from the Met Office.

Case study

Builders

I am having an extension done but my builder has stopped turning up. The work isn't finished and now I'm looking at it, he doesn't seem to have done a great job. What are my rights?

Your contract with the builder will be governed by the Supply of Goods and Services Act 1982. The builder is obliged to use materials of satisfactory quality and the work that he or his contractors carry out has to be done with reasonable skill and care. If the work he has carried out is not satisfactory, you have the right to have the work put right at no extra cost to you. This can be done either by the original builder or, if he is no longer available, a substitute builder.

If your builder is no longer turning up, you may need to get the work finished by another builder. The first step is to give your original builder a date for him to return to do the work. You should do this in writing and make 'time of the essence'. If he does not comply with that timing, then get three quotes and send these to the original builder, letting him know that you will be getting the job rectified and completed elsewhere.

If you do not hear from him, then you should choose one of the builders from your new quote and proceed to have the work done. Any extra cost over and above the original quoted price can be recovered from the original builder.

If your original builder has stopped trading, then it may not be possible to recover any extra cost for rectification and completion unless you have paid for some of the work by credit card.

If the standard of work is poor, you should inform the builder that you have lost confidence in his ability to do the work and then proceed through the quote stage to get someone else to finish the work.

WHAT TO DO IF YOUR BUILDER STOPS TURNING UP

If your builder disappears from the site to do other work, and stops returning your calls, then bear in mind that if you didn't agree a fixed completion date in your contract that under the Supply and Goods Services Act (1982), the builder must only complete the project in a 'reasonable time'.

Send a recorded delivery letter to the building company saying that you believe it has gone beyond a reasonable time, and that you are making 'time of the essence' now.

This basically asserts your right not to pay for the work if the service isn't delivered within the new timeframe that you're setting, as by invoking a 'time of the essence' order, you are now defining your contract with your trader mainly in terms of time.

Set a reasonable deadline for the work to be completed in what is known as providing notice, and explain that if this is not done, you will employ a second builder to complete the work and recover the additional expense from the original builder. Any important courses of action should always be put in writing – keep your correspondence simple and to the point.

If your builder doesn't respond or fails to pay if you have to employ another builder, you could take it to the small claims court, but this should be your last resort. Consider taking your complaint or dispute first to the builder or trader's regulating body, or consult legal advice on arbitration or mediation schemes to sort out the problem without incurring the expense or hassle of going to court. For more information on this subject, see pages 165–83.

2 PROFESSIONALS

- Accountants
- Architects
- Estate agents
- Financial advisers
- Solicitors
- Surveyors

CHOOSING THE RIGHT PROFESSIONAL FOR THE JOB

At some point in our lives, most of us will need to seek professional advice from an expert such as a solicitor, accountant, independent financial adviser, estate agent, surveyor or an architect. They may not come cheap, but they've trained for years to become experts in their field – or at least, that's what we'd like to think. In reality, there can be huge variations in the service you receive from so-called experts, while finding one with the specialisms you require can be time-consuming and tricky.

Choosing the right professional will make your life easier, while choosing a bad one could actually add to your stress levels, not to mention waste your money. To make sure the professional you pick is going to help rather than hinder your cause, carry out a few basic checks, and don't be afraid to ask any questions.

Starter checklist
▶ Start by asking around for recommendations from family or friends, or check Which? Local for recommendations in your area.
▶ Make a shortlist of at least three professionals and compare costs, experience and qualifications before making your choice.
▶ Read all the paperwork you're given carefully, and don't sign on the dotted line unless you agree to all the terms and conditions of service listed.
▶ Make sure you'll be hiring the right professional, who specialises in the sort of work you'd like to be carried out.

Choosing and checking
ACCOUNTANTS

Hiring an accountant is a rather grey area in terms of its financial necessity. If you are considering doing your own accounts to cut costs when you've just set up your business, weigh up how much time and money it will cost you to see if it's worth it. If you are going to be earning less than £10,000 in your first year of trading and have no employees, it probably isn't worth paying for the service. You can work out how much you're likely to earn in your first year after three months of starting your business by calculating an average monthly income for your first quarter, and multiplying this figure by four to get a likely estimate for earnings over the next nine months.

HM Revenue & Customs (HMRC) provide online tax self-assessment guides. You can check these out and register for self-assessment online at www.hmrc.gov.uk. Contrary to popular belief, you do not need an accountant to sign off your tax returns at the end of the year, and can do it yourself. However, time is money, and if you're not good with figures and don't have much of an eye for detail, it's worth seeking simple bookkeeping services from an accountant to avoid doing your own tax returns if you're earning over £10,000.

If you run any sort of business, you are legally required to keep certain records and deal with the following issues:

▶ Pay As you Earn (PAYE) if you have any employees, and VAT records if you are VAT registered.
▶ You must submit an annual tax return to HMRC.
▶ If your company has an annual turnover of more than £6.5 million, you will also need to appoint an auditor in order to carry out an annual audit of your accounts.

If you employ members of staff and are VAT registered, your firm's finances will get more complex. You will need advice on handling your payroll and dealing with VAT accounting; any firm you plump for will need to be equipped to deal with this. You can also find out if you've paid too much tax in the past on your business, and try to reclaim it.

If you think you've paid too much in Income Tax, ask your accountant to contact HMRC to amend your last tax return. If you think you're owed money, tell your accountant how you'd like to receive it – either as a cheque, or have the money paid directly into your bank account, or whether you'd like to save it to deduct the sum from your next tax bill. If you're owed less than £10, or you've got another tax bill due shortly, the latter may be the best option. Visit www.hmrc.gov.uk for more information.

HMRC does its own checks into tax returns to determine whether you're paying the right amount of tax – too much or too little – which can happen up to 12 months after the date when you submitted your return, and they may contact you for information, or go through your accountant. If you've paid too much tax, HMRC will change your tax return, and you'll get a repayment, which in some cases will have interest added onto it as well. This works the other way if you haven't paid enough tax.

You may be able to do some of this work yourself, but businesses and sole traders often prefer to use an accountant to share some of the burden. Accountants can suggest cost-cutting measures for your business, and keep you abreast of new financial legislation and changes in the law.

If you're seeking the services of an accountant to handle your business' finances, you'll probably be in the position where you will be paying at least 20 per cent of your business profits in tax and National Insurance, so it's worth investing your time in making sure the practice you'll be using is right for you. It may be one of the most long-term relationships you have in your business life – many businesses and individuals enjoy relationships of great longevity with their accountants.

Your accountant must have the relevant qualifications and experience to handle your affairs. Anyone can call themselves an accountant, but do they have the qualifications to back up their claim? And just as importantly, are they a member of any professional body?

There are six regulatory accountancy bodies in the UK, although accountants who offer services to individuals and businesses generally fall under two

Doing your own accounting?

If you're starting up your own business, it may be worth taking one of the short courses that HMRC offer for start-ups. These will cover aspects of accounting and tax, and give some tips on how you can prepare your accounts in a manner acceptable to HMRC. If your business turns over less than £15,000 in any year, you won't need to submit detailed accounts with your tax return. Visit www.businesslink.gov.uk/taxhelp for more information and to download a range of guides to help with your tax returns.

Limited company?

If your business is a limited company, you will also have to file accounts with the Registrar of Companies. For more information on this, visit www.businesslink.gov.uk to access a guide on how and when your annual accounts must be filed.

categories, Chartered Accountants (ACA/FCA as members are either Fellows or Associates of the Institute of Chartered Accountants in England and Wales, or ICAEW), and Chartered Certified Accountants (Association of Chartered Certified Accountants, or ACCA). Chartered accountants will have completed a three-to five-year training contract, and have passed the Institute's Professional Stage and Advanced Stage examinations. This equips them to process company accounts, handle and audit your tax affairs and handle corporate finance issues. As ICAEW members, they can also offer business advice to help your business improve its profitability, and potentially increase your market share if your business is big enough for this to be an issue.

Chartered Certified Accountants can also provide similar services, and have gone through an examination qualifying process with the ACCA, as in reality there is little difference between the two qualifications.

If you're hiring a bookkeeper for simple accounting, you should look to hire one who is a member of the Institute of Bookkeeping, and has undertaken examinations with the Institute. Visit www.bookkeepers.org.uk/FAQS for more information.

An unqualified accountant will possibly charge lower fees, but may not be able to match the standards of a qualified accountant. To find a list of practising chartered accountants, visit the Institute of Chartered Accountants in England and Wales' website at www.icaew.com for a full directory, or visit the ACCA at www.accaglobal.com to find chartered certified accountants online.

Key questions:
▶ *What areas of accountancy do you specialise in – simple bookkeeping or complex business advice?*
▶ *Will you remind me to get my accounts in before they are due, so I won't have to chase you?*

ARCHITECTS

As your home is likely to be the most valuable asset you possess, using an architect can radically enhance the appeal and value of your home, as well as your quality of life. Projects such as converting your ground floor living space from a few dingy, poorly-lit rooms into an open-plan oasis for light will improve your living situation drastically.

Equally, if you're a property developer and specialise in flat sales and lettings, employing an architect who will be able to, for example, convert your one-bedroom flat into a two-bedroom flat with en suite bathrooms by cleverly reconfiguring the space, you may be able to sell or rent your home for far more than previously.

It's essential to consult an architect if you're doing extensive building work, such as building as extension, converting your home into flats, or planning on a complete *Grand Designs*-style overhaul. You may find your home is more economic to run at the end of the project, and that the architect has made more effective use of the space than you might have thought possible. If your site is difficult to build on, or space is a serious issue, your architect may be able to come up with a clever, unique solution to make full use of your plot.

If you're planning extensive building works, an architect will have the experience to see your project through to completion, overseeing the design, going through the planning application process for you and making sure you're complying with Building Regulations (see Section 1), as well as managing your builders and making sure your project stays on budget. You should also be looking for them to manage the following:

▶ Obtaining competitive prices for the construction work.
▶ Monitoring progress on a regular basis through arranged meetings with your builder and construction team.
▶ Arranging and managing the input of other design specialists.
▶ Overseeing the coordination of the construction to completion.

Not all architects are suited to all jobs, as in any line of professional work. Some architects specialise in new building work or the commercial sector only, so it's important to establish early on whether the person you have approached is both experienced in small-scale domestic work, and is genuinely interested in taking on the project. Personal recommendation is one of the best ways of finding someone suitable, or it's worth buying self-build magazines such as *Grand Designs* or *SelfBuild & Design*, and looking at projects featured. All articles should include the name of the architect behind the project, if you come across a design you particularly like. You can also search the Royal Institute of British Architects' online directory at https://members.architecture.com to find an architect in your area.

Architects must be registered with the Architects Registration Board, which has a searchable database of 33,000 architects online at www.arb.org.uk. Many architects will also be members of the Royal Institute of British Architects (RIBA), the Royal Incorporation of Architects in Scotland (RIAS), the Royal Society of Architects in Wales (RSAW) or the Royal Society of Ulster Architects (RSUA).

Key questions:
▶ *What kind of work do you specialise in?*
▶ *Do you have enough experience to manage a team of builders?*

ESTATE AGENTS

In this high-tech day and age, it's now possible, should you wish to do so, to sell your own house online. If you decide to do this, you could save a lot of money, as the typical estate agent's fee is between 1.5 and 2 per cent. But the drawback is that you will have to put in a lot of time and work, arranging viewings and mediating with offers and your future buyer's solicitor yourself.

Plumping for an estate agent to handle all this remains the most popular option for UK sellers. Before hiring, make sure you go for one who specialises in selling properties similar to yours. You can check this either online, or by visiting the branch that will sell your home. It is pointless to expect much success if you have a stunning country house to sell from an agent who is used to dealing with small city centre flats, for example.

Estate agents don't need any formal qualifications to set up a practice, and have no requirement to pass exams or obtain a licence to do so either. This may account for the poor reputation estate agents have in the UK. But there are plenty of experienced operators who provide an excellent service, so the critical task is to find a good one. In a high street with six estate agents, only two or three may be right for you, so do some preliminary research by asking local people for recommendations, three at a minimum, or by checking agent ratings online at Which? Local.

Find out what estate agency qualifications your preferred agent and their staff possess. This may include NVQs in residential estate agency and the exam-based Certificate of Practice in Estate Agency offered by the National Association of Estate Agents (NAEA). Enquire, too, whether they are members of any associations, such as the NAEA. All estate agents must belong by law to redress schemes in the event of complaints such as those run by the Property Ombudsman (TPO) or the Surveyors Ombudsman Service (SOS).

Some estate agency practices are run by property surveyors, and these tend to have a good feel of the overall property market. As they will be members of RICS, they are likely to contribute to and receive their property price surveys. They also survey other properties locally, so tend to have a wider knowledge of individual local property prices. Visit www.ricsfirms.com to find surveyor-led estate agencies in your area.

Key questions:
▸ *What rate of commission will you charge for selling my home?*
▸ *What type of agency arrangement have I agreed to? Sole selling rights, sole agency, joint agency or multiple agency (see page 112)?*
▸ *How will you market my property – in your shop, on the internet, in the local press or by using just the 'for sale' sign board outside my front door?*

Estate agent codes of practice

Estate agents are unregulated, but trade associations they belong to have codes of practice and conduct for their members, and will handle complaints if you're unhappy with the services you have received. Members of the National Association of Estate Agents (NAEA) are bound by strict rules. The NAEA will take disciplinary action on your behalf if your agent hasn't protected or promoted your interests. Similarly, the Property Ombudsman (TPO) offers a similar service.

It is now mandatory for all estate agents to belong to an Ombudsman scheme so that complaints about them can be dealt with quickly and with more ease. Visit www.naea.co.uk and www.tpos.co.uk for more information.

Bear in mind that the Property Ombudsman will not usually review a complaint you may have about your estate agent until you've gone through the agent's own internal complaints procedure and not got anywhere.

FINANCIAL ADVISERS

You don't have to hire an independent financial adviser (IFA) to buy a financial product – you can also get advice from your bank or building society, insurance companies, mortgage brokers and stockbrokers – but if you don't, and you choose something unsuitable, you will have fewer grounds on which to make a complaint if your product doesn't work out. So it may be preferable to arm yourself with all the facts by consulting an IFA first before doing any of the following:

▶ If you want to start saving for a pension, or to get a mortgage.
▶ If you're looking to protect your family in the event of an accident, illness or death.
▶ If you're about to inherit a lump sum of money.
▶ If you're coming up to retirement and need help converting your pension fund into income for your retirement.
▶ If you're thinking about building your own home.

Not all banks and lenders will lend money for land, building work, converting or renovating property, so you will need to find a specialist lender to help you. A financial adviser could help you to unearth such a lender, and find a specialist company used to dealing with self-build, conversion and renovation projects.

There are two types of financial adviser. An IFA works independently, while a tied adviser works for a specific company, such as a bank. They will recommend their own company's products first and foremost, and often work on commission. This means they will receive a cut of the fee you pay for the product they recommend. In the past, this has led to conflicts of interest, where consumers have been recommended the wrong products because they have either knowingly or unknowingly paid their adviser via commission.

Depending on the type of help you need, there are different types of adviser that you may want to talk to. Often, consumers' first port of call if they want financial advice is their bank, or a life insurance company that sells investment products. But your bank or life insurance company is less focused on advice than on sales. This isn't good. Many aspects of financial planning require a savings scheme to be set up, or a life insurance policy purchase to protect a family from the worst. Not all advice should result in a sale. In fact, your financial adviser should assess your personal circumstances, and recommend only financial products that will be suitable for you.

What goes up can go down too

Bear in mind that while investing in shares can deliver growth, and give you the chance to reach your life goals faster than would be possible than leaving your money in a high interest savings account, the stock market can be volatile and turn nasty. Many would-be investors have been put off by the stock market falls of 2007 and 2008, when global share prices fell by 40 per cent. But according to the Barclays Equity-Gilt study, an annual look at the performance of different assets people might hold as investments, there is a 99 per cent probability of equities outperforming cash savings over as short a period as 18 years. So consider that if you're investing in stocks and shares, it should be with a long-term view in mind.

Most advisers are paid directly or indirectly by commissions on the products they sell. But not all financial products pay commission, National Savings & Investments is one example, which means it's less likely to be recommended.

Financial advisers may hold differing types of qualifications, but all should hold the basic Certificate in Financial Planning. Finding an adviser with a recognised qualification should be a top priority. It's illegal for an adviser to sell you a financial product if they aren't registered with either the Financial Services Authority (FSA) or the Personal Investment Authority (PIA).

The FSA is also planning to bring in new regulations in the future, when all advisers will need to have a minimum qualification that is equivalent to the first-year level at university, as the current certificate ranks roughly between a GCSE and an A level. You should be looking for something better than this. For more details of qualifications to see which exams come closest to your needs, go to www.which.co.uk/advice/financial-advisers/ifa-qualifications.

Key questions:
▸ *What area of finance do you specialise in?*
▸ *Are you paid by commission through the products you sell, or do you charge an hourly rate?*

Specialised financial advisers that you may want to consider, depending on your circumstances, are described overleaf.

Accountants: Accountants can also offer specialised guidance, especially on tax issues. Like solicitors (see overleaf), some have financial advice and planning qualifications. Their practices may include an IFA division, or they could refer you to an adviser.

Fund managers: For investors who don't have large sums at their disposal, or the time to research the shares they'd like to purchase, they can go into a collective investment scheme, also known as mutual funds. A fund manager makes the decision on what shares or assets to buy for the potentially thousands of investors on their books. If you don't have much cash to spare, your fund manager may offer you a regular saving option, where you can place several hundreds of pounds, or as little as £25 a month, in the fund.

Independent Financial Advisers (IFAs): IFAs are often specialists in various areas of financial planning. They are similar to mortgage brokers in that they can recommend financial products from the whole of the market. You can also discuss your investment strategy with them. An IFA should be reviewing your strategy with you on a regular basis to make sure you're on course to meet a particular goal. And if you're not, what you can change to make that happen.

Back to school for financial awareness

The huge range of financial products available on the market has made it increasingly difficult for consumers to develop much of a sense of financial awareness, or be very knowledgeable about products they are buying, such as mortgages or pensions, that may cost thousands of pounds. A recent survey by the Learning and Skills Council found that nearly nine out of ten consumers fail to understand basic financial calculations. The lack of awareness of what sub-prime mortgages are in practice, to name one notorious example, in part caused the recent banking crisis.

Financial education is now part of the school curriculum, but banks will soon be required to fund a new financial educational agency for adults, which will offer consumers personal finance advice. This includes information on how to calculate compound interest rates and understanding mortgage deals. It's currently the job of the Financial Services Authority (FSA) to provide financial education for consumers, but the job will be done in the future by a new and independent Consumer Education Agency.

Case study

Financial advisers

I have been to a financial adviser who has sold me a particular life insurance. I now find this insurance is not suitable for what I wanted. What can I do?

If you feel that your adviser has mis-sold you the life insurance policy, you will need to check whether your financial adviser is independent or tied to a particular insurance company. He/she should have informed you of their status at the outset. In addition, you should have been informed as to whether you would be paying for advice or if commission would be payable to the adviser by the insurance company.

If commission is payable then the amount of commission should be disclosed.

Your financial adviser should be regulated by the FSA, which issues guidance for the behaviour of its regulated members. If you believe that you have been missold your policy the first thing to do is to make a complaint to the adviser and their firm. If this does not solve the matter, then you can refer the complaint to the Financial Ombudsman Service who will adjudicate on the mis-selling.

In addition, you may be able to claim breach of contract and negligence.

Your financial adviser will have a contract with you for the supply of services. These services should be provided with reasonable skill and care under the Supply of Goods and Services Act 1982. This act is implied into contracts for the provision of services. If the adviser has not considered your requirements and advised you to take out an unsuitable life policy, then he has breached the contract and you will be entitled to damages for the breach, which would be the actual financial loss.

In addition, if you took out that particular policy because of something your adviser said to you, for example, you can have a waiver of premium if you are sick or unemployed and the policy does not provide for it, then you may be able to rescind the contract for misrepresentation. This means the parties would be put back in a position as if the contract had not taken place.

You may have a claim in negligence as the adviser owed you a duty of care. There may also be a claim in negligent mistatement.

For more information on this subject, see pages 165–83.

Mortgage advisers: The most common sources of information for mortgage hunters tend to come from lenders or mortgage brokers.

Lenders are usually only able to discuss their own range of products, which might not always be the most competitive. However, they operate under a set of rules set down by the FSA, which distinguishes between:

▶ Giving full advice as to which is the most suitable mortgage for the borrower.

▶ Providing a customer with information so they can reach a decision.

▶ Acting on an execution-only basis, so only providing you with the loan you asked for.

There are problems with these first two categories. The lender operates on the assumption that it has simply handed over information, enabling the decision to be made by the borrower, while some consumers believe they have been given 'advice' through this process.

Mortgage brokers abide by the same rules as lenders, but generally, you will be seeing a broker for advice, rather than looking to borrow money from the company they represent. A broker should be able to tell you about more than one lender's mortgages, using products drawn from several dozen providers. You get more choice by using a broker, and a better chance of finding a home loan to suit your needs. Many mortgage brokers are also financial advisers, but not all brokers who are financial advisers are independent. They may be tied to a handful of companies whose products they receive a commission to recommend and sell. Make sure you ask before taking their advice.

Solicitors: Many solicitors have financial advice qualifications, and their knowledge of the law is a definite asset for issues such as wills and Inheritance Tax (IHT). They can refer their clients to financial specialists and even IFAs.

Stockbrokers: If you are buying and selling shares regularly, you may need to speak to a stockbroker. They can act for you in three ways:

▶ On an execution-only basis, where you tell them what to invest in, or what to sell.

▶ On an advisory basis, where they will offer you their recommendations, but you will make the final decision.

▶ On a discretionary basis, where they have the power to make decisions on your behalf.

Brokers are similar to IFAs in that they give independent advice, and are answerable solely to you.

Wealth managers: Wealth managers specialise in investing your money, and make all decisions for it on your behalf. Their service is expensive, as any growth you enjoy must be at least the amount you've paid out – between 1.5 and 2 per cent of your total asset value – plus inflation to stand still. Their services tend to be restricted to investors with assets of at least £250,000.

SOLICITORS

Making sure you find the right solicitor who specialises in the right area of law is crucial. Firms may offer services in a variety of legal matters, including buying a home, making a will, setting up a business, renting your property, getting a divorce, making a personal injury claim, in addition to probate in the event of death.

The Law Society has an online directory to help you identify the type of specialist legal advice you may need. You can search for firms of solicitors based on their areas of law online at www.lawsociety.org.uk. Solicitors inform the Solicitors Regulation Authority (SRA) each year of the areas in law in which they specialise.

Crucial as it is to find the right person for the job, this can sometimes be tricky. For example, if you own a property with your partner, and decide to split from him/her, you won't be able to go to the high street property conveyancer who handled your purchase for you to handle the transfer of equity you require, as they will have little experience of anything other than conveyancing. In such a case, you would need to hire a solicitor with experience in family law, even if you have no children with your partner.

All solicitors working in private practice must hold a practising certificate issued by the Solicitors Regulation Authority, an independent regulator set up by the Law Society. This sets the rules that all solicitors must follow, and guarantees that the solicitor is qualified to practise law, and has professional indemnity insurance to protect you if anything goes wrong.

If you want to double-check that all is above board with your solicitor, you can ask to see their certificate, which should be proudly displayed in their office, or phone the Solicitors Regulation Authority on 0870 606 2555.

Find out if the firm you're looking to hire has received any quality awards, such as the Law Society Lexel quality award. You can confirm whether or not the firm has received such an award by phoning the Law Society on 020 7320 5933.

Key questions:
▶ *What area of law do you specialise in?*
▶ *Do you hold a Practising Certificate issued by the Solicitors Regulation Authority (SRA)?*

Executing a will

If a close friend or relative asks you to be the executor of their will, try to make sure you know its exact whereabouts. On the death of that person, you, as executor, will become responsible for administering the estate and applying for probate.

This can be a difficult area of law to get to grips with if you know nothing of it. 'Probate', or 'probate of the will', is a legal document issued to one or more people as the executors, which authorises them to deal with an estate. The Probate Registry must grant probate, which is known as the grant of representation, but can only do so after they've seen legal proof that you are the executor.

This grant of representation proves that you are entitled to claim the assets of the deceased, not for yourself, but in your capacity as personal representative. You will then be in a position to administer the estate, and must follow the will, and deal with the estate and beneficiaries according to the law.

When someone dies without leaving a will – recent research shows this could happen to as much as half of the population – you might discover that you are designated to be the administrator for that person's estate. If you are the next of kin responsible for administering this intestate estate, you will have to apply to the Probate Registry for letters of administration, which confirms you are able to administer the estate of the deceased relative.

Administrators must be the closest living relative to the deceased, and are chosen in this order:

▶ Spouse or registered civil partner.
▶ Children or grandchildren, if over the age of 18.
▶ Parents.
▶ Brother or sister, or their descendants if over the age of 18.
▶ Half brothers or half sisters, or descendants if aged over 18.
▶ Grandparents.
▶ Uncles or aunts, or descendants over the age of 18.
▶ Half aunts or uncles, or descendants over the age of 18.
▶ The Crown (the State) if no living relatives exist.

After an administrator has been appointed using this guide to priority, the Principal Probate Registry is your first point of contact. Either phone the helpline on 0845 302 0900, or visit www.hmrc.gov.uk/inheritance tax, and follow the links to probate. A useful guide to get hold of immediately is the form PA2, which is available to download from www.hmcourts-service.gov.uk. This form will enable you to sort out the deceased's estate affairs without legal help. After you've downloaded the form, click on the 'Forms and Guidance' tab on the website, and in the box 'Work type' go to 'Probate'.

It's important to distinguish between probate and letters of administration. Administrators have no legal authority to act until letters of administrators are issued to them, whereas executors may act immediately in the event of death.

When should you use a solicitor to administer probate?

There are some good reasons in favour of employing a solicitor – any number of complexities can arise with the administration of an estate. Consider also if you have time to cope with the legal side of an administration, or are you too busy? Potential issues may arise from the following:

▶ Errors: solicitors carry insurance in case they make mistakes. Another executor/ administrator who makes a mistake could be personally liable.

▶ If the deceased owned his or her own business, or was part of a family trust, a good knowledge of the law will be essential.

▶ In the event of intestacy, or if property is passed to children under the age of 18, a number of problems can arise.

▶ A situation that involves, on intestacy, an estranged relative who is entitled to a share in the estate. Relatives who have disappeared require careful handling, as does the situation if they aren't found.

▶ Homemade wills are a potential minefield of ambiguities. Legal help on their interpretation may be needed. An executor who wrongly interprets a will, or fails to distribute to a lawfully entitled beneficiary, could be financially liable for mistakes.

▶ If the will is contested, or there is a chance of anyone seeking a larger share of the estate under the Inheritance (Provision For Family and Dependants) Act 1975.

▶ If the deceased had significant debts. If you discover the estate is insolvent, don't continue with the administration and seek legal advice. Otherwise, you may become liable for the administrative costs and funeral expenses if you have authorised them.

SURVEYORS

There are many different types of surveyor, not all of whom will be qualified in the same lines of work. The main types who work in this field are:

Chartered building surveyors: They provide advice on property and construction, including the design of new homes or extensions, and the repair and restoration of existing homes. They conduct structural home surveys, which you may commission if you're buying a new property to assess its structural soundness. If you've decided to build your own home, you can commission a building surveyor (sometimes known as land surveyors) to do a land survey to check your plot for old mineshafts, quarries, and anything else that could dramatically raise the cost of your project. Building surveyors can also project manage major building work schemes. This includes handling applications for planning permission, providing advice on whether your design will meet the current Building Regulations (see Section 1), and inspecting the finished product at the end to ensure that it has. They will also handle the day-to-day management of the project, dealing with contractors, and making sure that deadlines are met.

Quantity surveyors (QS): QSs work from plans drawn up by an architect for self-build or big building projects to calculate what materials you'll need to do the work, and how much they will cost, and draw up what is known as a Bill of Quantities. They are also known professionally as cost consultants or commercial managers.

If you're looking to sell your home, you could commission a voluntary structural survey as part of a Home Information Pack (HIP) (see pages 104–5) to identify any major defects before you put it on the market. The same applies if you are buying a property, and want to make sure you know exactly what you'll be getting before buying – this may help you to negotiate on the price with the vendor if significant work needs to be done.

If you're building your own home and are searching for the perfect plot, talking to a land or buildings surveyor with an extensive knowledge of your local market could also help you to land your dream plot. Give your surveyor your list of criteria – for example, nicely situated plot away from busy roads that is surrounded by acres of open space – and ask them to inform you when anything suitable comes up for sale.

Surveys

If you're buying a home, you may want to use a surveyor for an independent survey to safeguard against any problems in the future, in addition to the basic survey commissioned by your lender. Surveys frequently identify faults that will allow you to negotiate on the price, so they very often pay for themselves. There are four types of survey: a homebuyer survey, a buildings survey, a home condition report (an optional feature of the Home Information Pack [HIP]), a buildings survey and a snagging survey.

A homebuyer survey will cost little more than £500, and will provide detailed information on the following:

▶ Roof, chimney, tiles and flashing.
▶ Walls, floors and ceilings.
▶ Guttering and drainage.
▶ Windows and doors.
▶ Structure and build quality.
▶ The location and its surrounding area.

A buildings survey is a more thorough assessment, which is suitable for older homes, and will go into more detail on, for example, the condition of timber and establish the presence of any pests. It's more expensive than a homebuyer survey, and will cost more than £500.

A home condition report is more detailed than a homebuyer survey. This would be commissioned as part of a HIP to give buyers a better idea of any underlying problems with the property; reports can also contain useful information on utility bills and council tax costs. But it doesn't include a valuation of the property, so until it does, it's best to use a homebuyer or buildings survey. Visit www.homeinformationpacks.gov.uk to see a sample report.

A snagging survey is specifically for new-build homes. New homes are covered by structural warranties issued by the National House-Building Council, Zurich (although Zurich no longer offers guarantees on new homes, you may be buying a property the developer has been selling for some time, which may still be covered by a Zurich guarantee or Premier Guarantee warranty). However, these only take into account the structure of the property. A snagging survey can cost from under £200 to £500, depending on the level of the service you need – there's a higher charge if negotiation with the developer on your behalf is required.

A fully qualified surveyor will have a degree or diploma accredited by the Royal Institution of Chartered Surveyors (RICS), and should have passed their Assessment of Professional Competence (APC) during their first two years of employment. Visit www.rics.org to find a surveyor in your area.

If you are doing any building works, it is key to hire a local surveyor as they will be aware of the planning guidelines and criteria set by your local planning authority. This could save you the disappointment and expense of a refusal or receiving back a long to-do list of the changes you will need to make.

Key questions:
▶ *What area do you specialise in?*
▶ *Will you be able to significantly decrease my build costs if I hire you to manage my building project?*

What should you ask before hiring?
ACCOUNTANTS

Before hiring an accountant, it's advisable to draw up a shortlist of at least three firms, and arrange to meet someone at each of these practices. Ask to speak to existing clients if possible, and obtain at least three references. Online reviews of accountants in your area are also available at Which? Local.

If you run your own business: The list of questions you should ask your accountant in a preliminary meeting should cover the following:
▶ Enter the meeting armed with your business plan. Does the firm offer the services you need to build your business?
▶ If you don't have a financial business plan, how much will they charge to draw one up?
▶ How many partners are there in the practice? Are they experienced in dealing with businesses of a similar size and nature to yours? What works for one business may not work for another, so it's crucial to establish that your accountant has a good understanding of your business sector and its needs.
▶ Do they hold professional indemnity insurance? Any accountant you hire should hold this, as it insures them if they make mistakes, or are negligent with your finances in any way.

▸ Do they provide personal financial advice as well?
▸ Take your accounting records with you. Can the accountant suggest any improvements?
▸ Who will be dealing with your work at the firm on a day-to-day basis?
▸ Will the service you receive be proactive? Will the practice remind you when you need to submit accounts, or send you updates on changes in tax law?
▸ How quickly will they respond to your queries?
▸ Does the firm offer any specialist services for businesses starting up, or on how to list your business on the stock market?
▸ If you need any audit, investment business or insolvency work doing, is the practice accountant authorised to take on this kind of work?
▸ How long has the firm been practising for?

If you are seeking one-off pieces of financial advice, or work as a freelancer or a contractor: The following questions apply:
▸ Does the firm have experience of working with other freelancers/contractors, or specialise in the type of advice you need?
▸ How much will you be taxed as a freelancer/contractor?
▸ When will you need to submit your accounts to pay your taxes? Will your accountant remind you when the deadline is looming?
▸ How much money should you put aside to pay your tax bill?
▸ What expenses are tax deductible?
▸ Will you need to register to pay VAT?
▸ How will you make National Insurance (NI) payments, and when are they payable?

Other checks: Check before you make your first appointment whether it is free of charge – specific advice may be billed for even at this early stage. Try to negotiate a free half-hour consultation.

Under the Money Laundering Regulations 2007, you'll need to take identification documents of two of the following with you to your meeting:
▸ Your passport or current driving licence.
▸ A utility bill which shows your name and address.
▸ Your National Insurance card.
Ensure the practice of your choice will be acceptable to any third parties involved in your business, such as investors, financial providers or shareholders to avoid any future problems or conflicts of business interests.

ARCHITECTS

Shortlist a number of firms via the RIBA website, Which? Local or personal recommendations. After you've done this, you should interview at least three architects to talk about your design to ensure they are familiar with the build design you want for your home, and have done similar work before. Ask to speak to past clients and ask to be shown examples of former work.

Hold a preliminary meeting before beginning any work – check if you will need to pay for this or if it will be free. Depending on the nature of your project, it can be helpful to take along photos of your home, along with any sketches and plans you may have drawn. You may also like to take along photos of buildings or design features you like that you have cut out from magazines.

It is important to establish at this stage what level of support you will require your architect to provide. The various stages involved in a typical building project include:

▶ Preliminary project-planning advice.
▶ Preparing drawings to your specifications.
▶ Submitting plans for local authority approval.
▶ Obtaining tenders for the work from contractors.
▶ Preparing contracts.
▶ Preparing work schedules.
▶ Supervising site work.
▶ Issuing certificates for payment.

The more of these services you use, the higher your bill will be at the end of the project.

Ensure your architect is up to date with the latest Building Regulations, or that the drawings they produce are passed by a building control expert before you submit your plans to the planning office. Architects are key in the process for gaining planning permission consent and for Building Regulations approval. It can delay your build project if the planners pass drawings that are then rejected by the local building control officer.

It is also advisable to draw up a brief with your architect as talks get more serious. You should address the following:

▶ What's the function of the finished product? What will it be used for, and by whom?
▶ State exactly what you want to achieve with your build project, both in the long and short term.

▸ What is your design direction? Can your architect work with your taste for modern or traditional design? Are you particularly into green materials and building methods? What sort of materials and finishes do you prefer? Make sure your architect will be using 3D software throughout the design process, as this will help you to visualise the project, and suggest any changes you'd like to make, far more than is possible than using paper plans. Ensure that your architect is aware of your budget from the start.

ESTATE AGENTS

Make sure that your preferred agent is advertising properties in the local paper and on the internet similar to the one you're selling. There is no point in asking one who usually sells large, expensive houses with land to market a small flat. Check, too, that your agent is based in a town as near as possible to your property and is already selling homes in your area.

Avoid choosing an agent using the 'board count' method, which means a vendor goes for the agent with the most 'For sale' boards in the area. The agent with the most boards is not necessarily the most successful at selling your type of property – they may be having a big push to increase their market share, or be pulling in their sellers (but not buyers) with misleadingly high property prices. Think about the following questions:

▸ How will your agent plan to advertise your property? Via its shop window, or by advertising in the local paper or online?

▸ Will your estate agent do weekend or evening viewings, and will you need to be present? If they don't, this could lose you many viewings, as a key portion of the homebuying market is made up of professionals who won't be able to view your home during the day if they're out at work.

▸ Do they charge for anything else other than agency fees? Always check the small print.

Your estate agent should also advise you that you won't be able to market your home until you've acquired a Home Information Pack (HIP), which should contain your home's title deeds, local searches and an energy performance certificate, which will rate your home's energy efficiency. This should cost in the region of £350. Your agent may offer to provide the HIP for you, but it could be cheaper to shop online, so compare the costs to get a better deal. Visit the Government's HIP website at www.homeinformationpacks.gov.uk for more information.

Ask your agent to reveal to you any financial interest that they have in offers made on your property. For example, they are not allowed to collude with property developers so that the only offers they give to you are ones that suit their interests.

The lowdown on HIPs

HIPs, which were introduced to the market in 2007, are a must-buy for homeowners looking to sell their properties – you can't put a property on the market without one.

But unfortunately, they're not as useful as they originally had the potential to be. The important Home Condition Report, legal summary and other specialist search documents aren't compulsory to include.

But on the plus side, if you're a first-time buyer, or don't have a property of your own to sell, you won't have to pay anything for the HIP if you're buying a home, and will get the benefit of the documents that are compulsory for free. The following items are compulsory:

▶ A HIP index checklist
▶ An energy performance certificate (EPC)
▶ Standard searches
▶ The title deeds
▶ A sale statement on the property's particulars
▶ Evidence of title
▶ Sustainability information for new-build homes
▶ If you are buying a flat, the HIP must contain a copy of the lease

You will also be able to use the HIP to negotiate on the price of the property – if it needs to be made more energy efficient, if it requires double glazing, for example, or if you need to have a water meter fitted.

The HIP may also contain the following information, which could affect how much you pay for the property, if you'll need to renegotiate, and how long it will take to purchase it:

▶ The area around the property could affect your decision to buy. For example, has the property ever been flooded before, or is it built on a floodplain?
▶ What exactly is included in the property sale? Will it encompass the garden shed or kitchen appliances? If appliances such as washing machines or dishwashers are included, you may want to offer more cash for the property or, if you don't want them or the owner wants to take them with them, you can offer less.

- Is the property leasehold, where you basically only buy the lease for a number of years, for example, 99 or 125 years? You will need to request information on annual service charges and ground rent, which could add thousands of pounds to your expenses each year. If the lease is much less than this – a property with less than 70 years left on the lease is hard to sell, as obtaining a mortgage for it is difficult – the current owner might need to extend the lease before they can sell the property.
- What are the boundaries around the property? Does the parking space outside belong to you or a neighbour?
- How is the home heated? Does it have a gas boiler, and has this been checked recently?
- How energy efficient is the property? What are its estimated utility bills?
- Is the property listed or in a conservation area?
- What Council Tax band is the property in?
- Does the property have full title deeds? If not, this could take weeks or months to register with the Land Registry.
- Is there anything else you need to know? Are your new next-door neighbours planning to build a large extension, or will a new road or a housing estate be built nearby?

Estate agents and HIPs – watch out for rogue traders

Before handing over any cash to your estate agent to pay for your HIP, ask them to provide a receipt for the cost from the HIP provider. The Law Society issued a recent warning that estate agents could be receiving hidden commissions on selling HIPs on to sellers after they've purchased them from a HIP provider. A Which? report in August 2009 revealed that some agents are charging sellers more than 50 per cent extra than the provider's cost of the report.

It's not a criminal offence for your agent to add their own commission to the costs, but it's disreputable for them not to declare openly to homeowners that they are taking a cut, and the practice has been condemned by the National Association of Estate Agents, who have threatened to fine agents taking undisclosed sums of up to £1,000 each time they do it.

If you're in any doubt, shop around and visit online HIPs providers such as www.hipsonline.co.uk to potentially save yourself hundreds of pounds.

FINANCIAL ADVISERS

Set up a preliminary meeting, checking whether or not you will be paying for it first, to see if your adviser will be able to meet your needs. The adviser should ask you questions about your financial circumstances and your future goals, assess your current financial situation and recommend suitable products accordingly. Go into the meeting armed with the following information:

▶ Details of any partners, children or other dependents.
▶ Proof of how much you earn, what rate of Income Tax you pay, and details of any financial products you may already have, such as pension plans and mortgages.
▶ Details of your current savings and where you have stashed any money away.
▶ Details of any debts you may have incurred.
▶ Think about your financial goals for the future. How much cash do you think you can afford to spare to reach them?

Think about how you feel about risk before the meeting. Ultimately, it's important not to risk losing any money you put in, but are you willing to accept the risk of a potential loss if it gives you the chance of a bigger return in the future?

During the meeting, your adviser should give you details of the services they offer, and the range of products they can advise on. Ask for details on how you can pay for the service, checking if they are commission-led. If you are meeting with a range of advisers, take the opportunity to shop around and compare what is being offered to you. Once your adviser has discussed your goals with you, they should give you a written recommendation of what products will be suitable. Make sure you obtain information about the products they may be offering, which should answer questions about:

▶ The product's aim, and how much you should expect in returns, and over what period.
▶ Your commitment to the product – how long will you be tied into it for, and over what period?
▶ Details on how your payments are invested.
▶ Any potential risks.
▶ Your tax position if you buy the product.

Read through all the information you're provided with to make sure the product is right for you. Always ask questions about anything you may not understand.

Make sure your adviser has experience in the field in which you need advice – pensions specialists won't be helpful if you need mortgage advice, for instance.

Avoid financial advisers who are paid using a commission from the products they sell to you. In the past, consumers have been sold unsuitable products by advisers who have been tempted to recommend schemes according to the amount of commission they receive from it, rather than determining what will be most useful to their client. Instead, go for one who sets an hourly rate, or charges a set fee for work – financial advisers must now offer consumers a method of paying for a service with fees only.

If you are paying by commission, make sure your adviser tells you how this is calculated – you should know what you are paying for, how much it will cost, and how you are paying for it. Ask if your adviser is tied in any way to a company, such as a bank. If they are, it's unlikely they will offer you advice on the best products on the market to suit your needs, so ensure your adviser is thoroughly independent before hiring.

Get a number of references before hiring anyone, and ask friends with business interests if they have been particularly well served by their advisers. Remember that their financial needs may be different to yours, however. Check Which? Local for recommendations in your area. Independent website www.mylocaladviser.co.uk verifies all financial advisers listed on its site against the FSA register on a monthly basis.

Stockbrokers

If you're looking to invest in the stock market, it's a better idea to create a portfolio of shares, rather than investing in individual companies. Unless you have a very good tip that one company's shares are likely to do extremely well, you should be looking to diversify your assets to reduce the overall risk of your investments, and their volatility.

You should be looking for your stockbroker to excel in the following areas:
▶ Quality of information. Do they have services that will help with your trading, such as price improvers, which scan the market to get the best price for your stock?
▶ Speed of action. Telephone and internet services could give you access to instant dealing, while postal executions take a couple of days.
▶ Markets available. Do they offer a wide range of investment products?
▶ Do they issue certificates or paperless shares? Most brokers hold shares for clients in paperless form, which allows deals to be paid for within three rather than ten days.

Newspapers, magazines and news websites are also a good way to find an IFA, working on the principle that if journalists, who should know something about the subject they're writing on, keep quoting a particular adviser in their newspaper or magazine, then that individual must be good. But bear in mind that some advisers are good at firing off an instant quote to a reporter, but not as good at serving their clients' needs.

SOLICITORS

After you've decided what sort of solicitor you'll need to speak to, it will be useful to shop around and obtain several quotes for the work you'll need doing, as charges will vary from firm to firm. Ask about references, and log on to Which Local? for recommendations in your area. The Law Society also has an online directory you can use to find a local solicitor at www.lawsociety.org.uk/findasolicitor.

When you've pinpointed a suitable firm, make an appointment to discuss the work you'll need doing. Most solicitors will charge next to nothing, or nothing at all, for a short preliminary interview. Ask if you should bring any documents with you, such as proof of identity and address, a current passport, driving licence or recent utilities bill. You'll need to prepare thoroughly for this first meeting, and do the following tasks well in advance:

▶ Make a list of the main points you want to raise, or questions you'll need to ask.
▶ Stack up any paperwork that might be relevant to your case, and put it in order so you can refer to it quickly.
▶ Have your notes in front of you, and tick off every point as it's covered. Don't be afraid to ask for explanations of any legal jargon you might not understand, or any information that seems confusing. Ask if you will need to provide any more information.

Language barriers
If English isn't your first language, and you don't feel comfortable in dealing with the complexities of the UK legal system outside your mother tongue, you should mention this to any solicitor you contact. If you give them enough notice, a firm can arrange for an interpreter to be present at your meetings.

Legal Aid

If you need help with legal costs if you are on a low income or are receiving benefits, you may be eligible for Legal Aid. You can ask your solicitor about applying for this. But be aware that not all solicitors take Legal Aid cases. Find out if you are eligible by contacting your nearest Citizens' Advice Bureau or law centre. You can search for solicitors who take on Legal Aid cases at the Community Legal Service website at www. clsdirect.org.uk. Legal Aid is managed by the Legal Services Commission, which works to ensure that all firms offering this meet high standards of quality.

Check beforehand how long the interview will last so you manage to squeeze in all the points you need to cover. Find out, if relevant, if you are eligible for Legal Aid (see above). When the interview draws to a close, ask the solicitor you've dealt with to send you a letter summarising the advice you've been given, and to confirm the following:

▶ That the solicitor you have seen will take on the work, and the name of the person in their firm who will be dealing with your case.
▶ The amount of time it will take.
▶ Cost estimates and details on any agreed spending limits.

Check if any costs can be fixed to a spending limit – they often are in simple conveyancing cases, for example. If the costs you incur look likely to go over this limit, ask your solicitor to contact you to notify you of this, and to get your agreement to continue with the work.

It's important that you feel comfortable with the person who will be dealing with your case, particularly if you're seeking representation on a personal matter. In the event of a relationship breakdown, many individuals prefer to deal with someone of the same sex, for example. Don't be scared to say that you would feel more comfortable with this.

On the street where you live?

If you're elderly, ill or disabled, you may wish to hire a firm close to where you live. Some solicitors are happy to make home or hospital visits, so if travelling is an issue, it's well worth asking for this service.

If you've gone to a solicitor seeking financial advice, and they recommend an IFA to you, bear in mind this could be part of a commission-sharing agreement the two are participating in. Just because you are referred to an IFA by a solicitor doesn't automatically guarantee the adviser will be any good.

Ask your solicitor if they have any such agreements with IFAs. The Solicitors Regulation Authority (SRA) issued new guidelines in July 2009, which advises solicitors to only refer clients to independent advisers for financial advice, noting that referrals as part of a commission-sharing agreement breach the SRA's code of conduct.

SURVEYORS

The same criteria as listed on pages 111–12 for architects also applies to hiring a surveyor. If you're looking to build your own home, ask your surveyor if you will need to get planning permission from your local planning department before you purchase any plot. Ask your surveyor to visit the land and to check if any previous planning applications have been lodged on it and rejected.

If you've commissioned a building survey from a surveyor while purchasing a house, read it very carefully. Surveys often recommend specialist inspections of particular problems. Always follow these up. Traders will often give you a more accurate estimate for free, and you can get timber and damp surveys for nothing from firms specialising in their treatment.

What legal issues should you be aware of?
ACCOUNTANTS

Once you've found the right accountant for the job, the firm will send out a letter of engagement. This contract should clarify in detail your responsibilities, your accountant's responsibilities, what the fees will be for these services and how and when you will be charged.

Carefully check any terms and conditions laid out in the contract, in case there is a notice period that you must honour. Fixed-term contracts aren't very common in the world of accountancy. They tend to be open-ended and can be ended by you at any time. If you're not happy with the services your accountant provides and decide to switch, you will need to end the agreement with them before you sign an agreement with a new one. Check the terms and conditions of your contract to see how much notice you would be obliged to give to end your agreement, and then send in a letter to end your business relationship.

If you haven't settled payment under the agreed terms and conditions of the contract, your accountant has the right to withhold your figures and other data they may hold about your business.

ARCHITECTS

When setting down the services your architect is providing in writing, ask them to talk you through your rights as a consumer, under the terms of the Unfair Terms of Consumer Contracts Regulations (1999). Your architect should discuss this with you so that the terms of your agreement are clear, and 'individually negotiated in good faith'. It's crucial to be aware of these in case the work you need your architect to do significantly increases in what is known professionally as 'scope creep', either by necessity or choice, and costs rise and timeframes for completing the work are extended. Your contract should record:

▸ The details of your project, and the services your architect is providing.
▸ Calculations of fees and expenses.
▸ Details of the architect's insurance cover, and the period of liability this will extend over.
▸ Details of dispute resolution procedures.
▸ Information on the appointment of any other consultants working on the project.
▸ Who signs off day-to-day decisions on design, costs and other issues that may arise on site during the build process.

The RIBA can provide a Conditions and Schedule for a Domestic Project document. This outlines the following responsibilities of the architect:

▸ To perform the services required using reasonable skill and care.
▸ To act as your representative.
▸ The need to advise you on compliance with statutory requirements.
▸ A duty to make sure you're updated on the build's progress and on matters affecting time, cost and quality.

▶ Not to make any changes to the services provided or the design of the project unless in an emergency.

▶ Not to subcontract any of these obligations under the contract's agreement.

You can purchase a single copy of this agreement for £30 at www.ribabookshops.com. When you've ironed out all the details, your architect will draw up a Letter of Agreement for you both to sign.

ESTATE AGENTS

You can avoid running into difficulties with your agent by reading the contract they give you, which sets out their terms and conditions, and by re-negotiating anything you don't like before you sign. If you don't understand certain terms in the contract, don't sign it – you may be better off with another agent. Read the contract carefully and make sure you're familiar with the terms of sole, joint or multiple agency, which are defined as follows:

▶ A 'sole selling agent' will have an exclusive right to sell your property and will be paid even if you find a buyer for your home yourself.

▶ A 'sole agency' is still the only agent selling your home, but they won't be paid if you find your own buyer.

▶ Both of these options cost less than employing joint (two) or multiple agents, who will charge a higher commission to compensate for the fact that only one of them will get paid. It may be worth having more than one agent if your property is located between two towns because between them they will market your home more widely.

If the contract contains the term 'ready, willing and able purchaser', this means you'll have to pay the agent for finding a buyer, even if you decide to withdraw your property from sale. Don't sign the contract if it contains this term.

Bear in mind that if you give your agent sole agency, you will be locked into a contract for a certain period of time. It's best to have a break clause after six or eight weeks, and then if you're not satisfied, you will be able to go to another agent.

Check, too, if the contract is an open-ended agreement. Some agents insist that you will still have to pay them if a buyer they introduced to you buys your home within six months of a contract ending. Some say that you will have to pay no matter how long it is after the termination of your contract.

FINANCIAL ADVISERS

Contracts tend not to be signed with IFAs and stockbrokers and you are generally free to terminate the work that's being done whenever you wish. If you are given any paperwork to sign, check the terms and conditions to avoid being tied into a particular financial product for longer that you want to be.

If you've taken out a mortgage with a mortgage broker, you aren't committed to the mortgage until you exchange contracts with the buyer or seller of your home, although some providers require you to pay a penalty for cancelling the mortgage, or a deposit to guarantee their income in case the deal falls through.

If you buy any home or income-insurance products from your broker, they may ask you to sign a fee waiver agreement. This means they won't receive any fees from you for selling you the insurance products, but they will receive a commission from the insurance provider, as by signing the agreement, you will be committing to the product for a certain period of time – two years, for example. Check the small print on this to see how long you may be tied in for.

SOLICITORS

Whatever your case, you won't be tied into an agreement with your solicitor and are free to terminate the work at any point. Check the terms and conditions your firm will set out in their letter confirming they've taken on your case to see what fees you will have to pay if you terminate the work before it is completed.

Bear in mind that if you're hiring a solicitor on a 'no win, no fee' basis, they won't charge you costs if they lose (although you may have to pay the other side's costs), but if you win the case, you will generally need to pay a 'success fee' or commission as a percentage of the amount of compensation that you've won. This can be paid in two ways – either as a set 'success fee' or an agreed percentage of the compensation you receive. The 'success fee' will depend on your type of case – in road traffic accidents, the maximum that can be charged is 12.5 per cent of the solicitor's normal fee, while there are fixed success fees for claims made against employers, or for some personal injury claims. If there is a trial, the fee will be twice the solicitor's normal fee. If you are paying a direct percentage of your compensation payment, the Law Society recommends a maximum charge of 25 per cent, although it's common for solicitors to charge half of this percentage.

Property pledges

If you are selling your home, you will usually hire a solicitor/conveyancer to act for you after you have accepted an offer. They will draw up your contract of sale. Read it thoroughly before signing; it should be in two parts and cover the following areas:

▶ The particulars of sale, which describe the property and give the lease/freehold terms.

▶ The conditions of sale, which include your proposed completion date, and what deposit will be required on exchange of contracts with your seller/buyer.

The firm will send the same contract to your buyer's solicitor with copies of your home's title deeds.

Before hiring on this basis, establish how much you will need to pay from your compensation if you win to avoid any nasty surprises later on. Your solicitor should give you a conditional fee agreement to sign, which sets out the details of how much you will pay if you win.

SURVEYORS

As with architects, your surveyor should inform you of your rights as a consumer under the terms of the Unfair Terms of Consumer Contracts Regulations (1999),

Depending on the work you've commissioned from your surveyor, the RICS has a range of contracts for sale at www.ricsbooks.com/contracts, whether it's for design and build work, or minor, intermediate or standard building contracts in line with the Joints Contracts Tribunal (JCT). Your contract should also contain the following details, similar to those outlined in the architect section:

▶ The details of your project, and the services your surveyor is providing.

▶ Calculations of fees and expenses, and the commission your surveyor will take from the total build cost.

▶ Details of the surveyor's insurance cover, and the period of liability this will extend over.

▶ Details of dispute resolution procedures.

▶ Information on the appointment of other consultants working on the project.

▶ Who signs off day-to-day decisions on design, costs and other issues that may arise on site during the build process.

COSTS AND TIMESCALES

As with employing any type of professional, costs will vary according to your area and the level of expertise of the firm you're instructing. Many professionals charge an hourly rate (with the exception of estate agents who receive a percentage of the overall price your home has sold for), which can easily run up far beyond the original estimate you were given for the job. Hourly rates also fail to work as an incentive for professionals to work quickly on your case or project – after all, the more hours they spend on it, the more they will get paid. If in doubt, check with their respective professional association in relation to professional costs.

Ask before commissioning any work if there is any way your professional will either cap the amount you'll be spending with them, or will work on a fixed fee for a specific project – bookkeeping and conveyancing are often billed on a fixed fee basis, for example. If this won't be possible, ask if you can review the services you receive after a certain period of time, say a year, or when costs go beyond what you're prepared to spend to ensure you're receiving value for money.

Costs

ACCOUNTANTS

Accountancy fees will vary widely depending on the nature of your business, and the firm you engage to do the work for you. Basic bookkeeping and simple tax returns will cost little more than between £200 and £300 a year for sole traders, but if your business affairs are more complex, it could cost you upwards of £1,000.

Establish what these fees are, and when they will be payable. It may be possible to put a cap on the fee for your work for the first year as you start your business – investigate the charges and what they cover thoroughly and find out if you can negotiate a fixed fee.

Be sure to keep your accountant up to date on changes or problems in your business, or in your personal circumstances.

ARCHITECTS

There are no standard fees for hiring an architect – the cost will reflect the level of personal service you'll receive, and the amount of bespoke design your project involves. Based on independent surveys by the Royal Institute of British Architects (RIBA), the general cost of an architect's fees is between 8 and 12 per cent of the construction costs, but they can also charge a flat fee or an hourly rate. Fees for preparing your design and submitting it as a planning application are generally between 3 and 5 per cent of construction costs, according to an independent survey of architect's fees carried out in 2006 by Mirza & Nacey Research. The size of the practice, its reputation and specialist skills they have to offer will also affect the rate you're charged.

But in general, an architect will quote his/her fee as a percentage of the building cost or as a lump sum. Where the level of work is uncertain or for services such as surveys or party wall advice, you'll be quoted an hourly or a daily rate, along with an estimate of the amount of time he/she need to spend on your project. Travel costs, fees for copying drawings and documents and for making planning or Building Regulations applications will be billed for separately.

Try to pin down your architect to giving you an estimate of the total renovation costs, or build costs if you are building your own home. At the design stage, you will need to pay a third of the fee, another third during the construction information stage, and the final third during or following the start of building work on site, although it is advisable, as mentioned in Section 1, to keep back a contingency fund of between 10 and 20 per cent in case the costs start to rise.

Architects tend to issue their invoices monthly, but see if you can make regular payments over a different period of time if you prefer, or you may arrange to pay your architect on the completion of each stage of the work.

ESTATE AGENTS

Estate agents generally charge sellers a percentage of the final selling price, which is payable when the property is sold. Rates vary, but typically range between 1.5 and 1.75 per cent for sole agency, and 2–3 per cent for joint or multiple agency, plus VAT. It is worth trying to negotiate on the rate to see if you can shave a bit off.

Bear in mind that if you have given your agent sole agency – which awards them with the exclusive right to sell your property – you will be locked into a contract for a certain period of time. It's therefore best to have a break clause after six or eight weeks, and then if you're not satisfied, you will be able to go to another agent.

Check if the contract you signed on first engaging your agent is an open-ended agreement, or if you will need to pay your agent commission if they have introduced a buyer to you, but did not actually initiate the sale (see page 112).

Choose an agent who will give you a few days to allow the money you have received from the sale of your property to enter your account before charging interest on the amount you owe them. Also make sure your estate agent will require paying when the sale is completed rather than when contracts are exchanged. Don't give authority to pay the estate agent to anyone who isn't buying the property with you. This is known as irrevocable authority, and may affect your rights. If you have a complaint about the service provided, you won't have the power to withhold payment.

FINANCIAL ADVISERS

There are three ways in which you can pay for investment advice:
▶ Fees. You will pay the adviser a specific rate, which will either be an hourly fee or a set rate.
▶ By commission. Here, you pay the adviser indirectly through commission, which is deducted by the product provider from the package you purchase from them.
▶ Fees and commission. A combination of paying through fees and commission. To be assured that you're getting the best service and being offered the right range of products for you, it is preferable to pay your adviser fees out of your own pocket.

Most advisers offer all three payment options, but more than 80 per cent of advisers' payment currently comes from commission-led sales and many consumers believe that commission-led advice is free. However, advisers are now obliged to allow consumers to pay for a service or a product through fees only, so ask your IFA how they will receive payment for the service.

Make sure the adviser you want to employ offers the payment option that will suit you. If you are paying your adviser through commission, ask how this is calculated. If you're getting advice on your investments, ask your adviser if the price you've been quoted includes a review of your investments over time, or if you have to pay separately for this service.

The FSA is aiming to put an end to commissioned-based financial advice by 2012 to help consumers distinguish between advisers and salespeople. In recent years, the lines have become somewhat blurred, and many consumers have wound up with products that aren't right for them. Commission hasn't yet been completely outlawed, but the FSA advises that if an adviser recommends a product carrying commission, this should be made clear to the client.

If you are paying your IFA a fee, be prepared to fork out between £120 and £350 an hour for your adviser's time. Check whether this includes VAT.

Fund managers: Fund managers charge up to 5 per cent for each contribution you make, plus a further 1–1.5 per cent in annual management charges. There are further fees on top of this, so it's important to establish what these are from the outset to make sure it's worth it by working out how much you are likely to gain over, for example, a year, and weighing up your gains against your costs.

Stockbrokers: If you go for a full advisory service with your stockbroker, you will pay handsomely for it. Your portfolio will be monitored regularly, and your broker will be in regular contact with suggestions of shares to buy or sell. It will cost at least £1,000 a year or more, and is only worth considering if you have assets greater than £100,000.

A discretionary service, where a broker may buy and sell shares for you without getting your permission first, can also be very expensive. An execution-only service is a cheaper option, as the broker won't provide you with any advice, but simply take your order and place it for you. An internet-based, execution-only service is even cheaper, as it feeds orders directly into automated systems. Brokers acting in this manner can handle large volumes of share requests, and the costs associated with each order are lower. For the cheapest broker, you will pay at least £7 per order, and £10–12.50 using a broker offering a wider range of services. Other fees you may be charged can be for registration, custody and transfer-out fees if you move to another broker, in addition to charges for issuing stock certificates. A £1 fee is also levied on all transactions over £10,000, and stamp duty charged at 0.5 per cent of the value of your share prices, or 1 per cent for Irish stocks.

Wealth managers: These advisers charge an initial fee to act for you of 1.5–2 per cent of your assets at the point of investment, followed by an annual charge of around 2 per cent. Some levy additional dealing costs of up to 1 per cent, but these won't be charged on your whole portfolio. Most wealth managers say they will buy and sell around a third of a client's portfolio each year.

SOLICITORS

Solicitors won't always charge a fixed fee for a particular job. Your bill will often be worked out on an hourly basis – the longer it takes, the more it will cost. This

---

No sale, no fee

If you are buying a property, you could consider hiring a solicitor/conveyancer who works on a 'no sale, no fee' basis. Conveyancers who take on too many cases are often forced into a 'fire fighting' approach to their work – they pick up a file, realise something is missing, request the information, and won't chase it again for a week. Delays of this kind can lead to failed sales.

Taking a 'no sale, no fee' deal gives conveyancers an incentive to do the job quickly, and reduces the chances of hold-ups as they are more likely to get paid for finishing the job. Most 'no sale, no fee' firms offer 'fixed-fee' conveyancing, which means you will only pay the price you agree to initially. So the more efficient your conveyancer is, the more likely they are to make a profit. Potentially the opposite of those solicitors who charge by the hour!

Probate fees

A solicitor's fees for dealing with an estate are paid for out of the deceased's property. The executors or administrators don't have to pay for them out of their own pockets, along with any other debts or taxes – any costs incurred are usually paid first from the assets of the estate, after which the remaining cash is distributed among the beneficiaries.

Solicitors should charge fees in accordance with the Solicitors' (Non-Contentious Business) Remuneration Order 2009. This sets out elements that will affect the final fee, including the time spent, the complexity of the estate and its value. Obviously, charges will be less for a straightforward transaction than for a more complex case, although the solicitor won't necessarily know if complications will arise from the outset. Ask your solicitor how often you will be advised on the probate's progress – bear in mind that you will be billed for each letter or phone call.

can range from £60 to £400 upwards an hour. Court costs and other fees are usually on top of this (these are known as disbursements), as well as VAT.

For other types of cases, such as personal injury, many solicitors are prepared to work on a conditional fee basis. This is the type of work promised in many TV adverts, on a 'no win, no fee' basis (see also page 113). If you win the case, the other side will cover your solicitor's fees, although your solicitor is

For the public good

If you don't qualify for free Legal Aid (see page 109 for more information), it's worth considering finding a solicitor who will act for you as part of pro bono work. A phrase derived from Latin meaning 'for the public good', this term is used to describe professional work done voluntarily by solicitors as a public service, and is done to ensure access to justice for the less affluent. Recently, pro bono work has encompassed cases ranging from providing advice and representation for asylum seekers with no funds to running free legal advice clinics, or providing mediation advice for individuals involved in disputes who don't want the expense of going to court. Visit Law Works (run by the Solicitors Pro Bono Group) at www.lawworks.org.uk for more information on pro bono work.

likely to take a cut of any financial settlement you receive. If you lose, you won't have to pay your solicitor's fees, but it may be worth looking in to taking out an insurance policy to cover the other side's costs if you lose. This 'no win, no fee' precedent can apply to other types of law too, so it's worth checking if the firm you've picked will take a case on this payment basis. Full payment is generally due when the case has been resolved, but you may be asked to pay a deposit in advance.

SURVEYORS

Ask your surveyor to estimate how much renovation costs will run to, or if you're building your own home, what the total bill will be – like architects, they tend to take a percentage of the total cost. What this percentage is depends on their involvement in your project. If they've designed the project, managed it and have managed your costs, this figure is likely to be between 10 and 12.5 per cent of the agreed final amount. But if you take the design element out of the service, you should pay between 6 and 8 per cent.

The Royal Institution of Chartered Surveyors (RICS) no longer publishes recommended fee scales or guidance on fees, so whatever fee your surveyor charges is negotiable. However, rates and hourly charges, if your surveyor is charging an hourly rate for smaller pieces of work, will vary, the RICS confirms, ranging from £60 to £85 an hour in a medium-sized practice outside of London to engage a senior surveyor, going up to £95–£125 an hour if you've engaged a partner in the practice. This estimate rises to between £75 and £95 an hour for a senior surveyor in London, and £100–£150 to engage a partner.

Timescales and schedules
ACCOUNTANTS

Your accountant may charge a monthly fee for their services, provide their services at an hourly rate, or if the work you need doing isn't complex, it may be a one-off payment at the end of the tax year. Check how often fees will be billed, and remember you can negotiate if you're not happy with the timeframe they provide for you.

It's important to keep in touch with your accountant throughout the year, rather than just frantically contacting them when your year-end books are due. When your accounts have been prepared, you should receive a letter setting out any future tax liabilities.

ARCHITECTS

As with all building work, even if you have an architect to supervise your project for you, the process will be unpredictable and potentially beset with difficulties. Work may not always proceed as you've planned, but if you have a clear idea of the order in which work should be taking place, this will at least give you a rough guide to work with. At least if you are hiring an architect to manage the project, the contract between the architect and contractor will include penalties for late completion, which is more likely to keep everyone on course.

Just as with employing a builder, you will need to have broken down the job into itemised phases, within a timescale agreed with your architect, who should have produced a programme of events for you, with the time taken or end date stated. Make sure you know exactly when critical stages of your renovation or build project will be carried out, such as the plumbing installed or the breaking through into your home from an extension.

ESTATE AGENTS

Keep in regular contact with your agent and don't disappear for a long weekend or a holiday without letting them know. Agree on a time to receive regular updates on how your home is faring on the market. Your home should receive interest or potential offers when it has been on the market for an average of eight weeks. If it hasn't caused much of a stir, ask why not. There could be a problem with your agent's valuation, or the marketing of your home, and how it has been advertised for sale. Consider revising your asking price. Ask your agent if prices have dropped locally, and what similar properties are selling for. How much of a price drop would attract interest?

If your agent isn't very helpful, and you have negotiated a break clause after six to eight weeks in your contract, consider hiring another agent. You may have more luck with your sale elsewhere.

Accepting an offer

When someone makes an offer on your property, there are a number of things to consider other than whether the price is right. The buyer's financial position is also crucial, as is how quickly they can move. If your estate agent is any good, they should be able to offer you advice on the quality of the buyer and the offer.

Legally, agents must pass on all offers on a property, promptly and in writing. Get your agent to check that the buyer is serious and has his/her finances in place before you take the property off the market.

Beware of being pushed into accepting a low offer. If it is way below your asking price, consider that although you are paying your estate agent, they will only receive money for their services if the property sells, so their motives may not be entirely pure for pushing you to accept any sale.

FINANCIAL ADVISERS

Depending on the work you've arranged with your IFA, mortgage broker or stockbroker, the timescale for your work may be short- or long-term. Arranging a mortgage should only take one meeting, face to face, with your broker after they've run a credit check on you, but your relationship with your IFA or stockbroker could be of a much longer duration.

If you are buying a property at auction, which requires you to complete on the purchase within 28 days, you will need to find a broker who can arrange a mortgage at very short notice to avoid losing your chance to buy the property.

Draw up a plan of action with your IFA or stockbroker stating how long you want to invest your money or assets, and make sure you review how your investments are going with them at least on a quarterly basis.

Fund managers: You will need constantly to assess how your assets are changing over time with your manager. This is crucial, regardless of whether stocks are rising or falling. When stocks are falling, review them to ensure your portfolio is placed on the defence – this could mean moving out of sustainability shares and into, for example, food retailers. When stocks are rising, check again to see that your portfolio is well placed over a wide range of assets.

You should be looking to hire a fund manager with research expertise as well as skill. A good manager should be researching the businesses they're investing in regularly, as well as having the experience to trade day in and out, and selling and buying shares when needed.

Check how many shares the fund you're thinking of investing in has – according to a mandate that sets the guidelines for managers about how they should invest consumers' money, this should be between 20 and 100 different company shares.

Find out exactly which investment area your money is dealing with – is it in bank shares, Africa or in sustainability? This should be clear because the mandate is set out, but make sure you're aware of what your money is going into from the off.

Fund managers tend to switch jobs at least every four years. You should check not just the fund when hiring but also the manager's performance with different funds. Online investor information website Citywire assesses fund performance at www.citywire.co.uk.

Bear in mind that many funds often invest not just in the same sector but in the same companies. Ask your adviser to recommend funds where the investment style of each manager is distinct, and where investments are diversified.

SOLICITORS

Your solicitor should consult you at every important stage throughout your case to check how you want to proceed. They should keep you informed of progress and costs, even when there are no significant developments.

Again, if you are buying a home at auction, you will need to have hired a solicitor or conveyancer who will be capable of handling your case within the 28 days you have to purchase the property. You should have made your time constraints on this clear when employing your solicitor.

You will need to do your bit too on the communication front, and tell your solicitor about any changes to your personal circumstances which might affect your case. This also includes alterations to your financial position, which could change your eligibility for Legal Aid if you are claiming it.

Probate

An application for a grant of probate won't be accepted within seven days of a death, or letters of administration within 14 days. If there is a will and all the information is there, with the required Inheritance Tax (IHT) liability (the known taxable value of the estate) in place, your application could be dealt with in two weeks. It could be all done and dusted in three to four weeks if everything is clear.

Life is rarely this simple, however, and some estates can take months to sort out. Any of the following could delay the process:

▶ A post-mortem is required.
▶ One of the executors isn't available.
▶ The will is nowhere to be seen or its contents are ambiguous.
▶ Your solicitor is too busy to give the matter priority.
▶ Property has to be transferred.
▶ Someone may make a claim against the estate – they have six months from the awarding of the grant to begin proceedings. Time should be allowed for claimants to come forward.
▶ A dependant child, ex-spouse or civil or other partner is thinking of making a claim.
▶ Valuations of any shares held by the deceased have to be obtained, but the share certificates have gone missing.
▶ The deceased made recent gifts of money or property, but no one knows the exact details.
▶ The deceased received a payment from an old family trust every year, but the trustees of this fund haven't made a tax return for the past two to three years.
▶ One or more of the beneficiaries can't be found, or may have died.
▶ The deceased's family can't decide what to do with the deceased's primary residence.
▶ A tax return is required up to the death of the testator.

SURVEYORS

As for employing architects, it is as well to be aware of the fact that the work might not proceed as you had hoped. Having a clear order of events written down will help you work your way through any problems that might arise.

3 MISCELLANEOUS TRADES

- Antiques restorers
- Car mechanics
- Chimney sweeps
- Computer repairers
- Drains specialists
- Locksmiths
- Piano tuners
- Removal firms

FINDING THE RIGHT
TRADESMAN FOR THE JOB

W hen it comes to employing miscellaneous tradespeople, such as chimney sweeps, locksmiths, drainage specialists or car mechanics, the task can be a daunting one.
Some of these trades, such as furniture restoration, are perceived as being a little outdated, although they are still very necessary. As public awareness of some of the trades mentioned here is often limited, if you don't know how to go about hiring the best person for the job, or even what the job should entail, you're leaving yourself to the mercy of rogue traders – the bane of all the trade associations mentioned in this section.

The Office of Fair Trading recently reported that it has received a record number of complaints about rogue traders, up by 18 per cent since 2008. This has cost householders a massive £8 million, the result of sole traders looking to earn a quick buck in the recession by taking advantage of public unawareness about the right questions to ask specific traders. This section will help you to avoid being stung and, even worse, causing permanent damage to your home or precious possessions.

Choosing and checking
ANTIQUES RESTORER

If you're the proud owner of antique furniture, an old painting or an old tapestry that needs a little reconstruction work, it is advisable to hire a specialist to do the job. Anything at all complex requires a trained eye upon it before work begins, and if you attempt a repair yourself, you could do permanent, irreversible damage to your prized possessions, affecting them both in value and appearance.

But finding the right person to restore your goods will also be something of a challenge, and one that must be handled with as much care as your antiques. Antiques restoration is a complex and academic business. To do it properly, specialists need a thorough knowledge of the history of a wide range of furniture and restoration methods, and should hold degrees or diplomas in the conservation and restoration of antique furniture. They may have specific City and Guilds qualifications in cabinet making, restoration and traditional upholstery.

Membership of a trade body is also a must. To join the main trade body of antique restoration, the British Antique Furniture Restoration Association (BAFRA), entrants must have the following:

▶ Five years' experience in the profession, and four years for BAFRA Associate Graduate members.

▶ A thorough knowledge of furniture history.

▶ Two references from clients who are themselves knowledgeable about furniture (BAFRA also checks their credentials as referees).

▶ Skills in cabinet making and finishing, in addition to more specialist skills such as gilding, boullework, oriental lacquerwork, textile conservation, metalwork, upholstery and seat weaving.

Applicants' workshops are visited by a BAFRA assessor to test their skills and knowledge as well as their integrity, which in this context relates to an understanding that furniture and other objects should be kept to their original form if possible, and changed as little as is necessary. Members undergo a reassessment every three years to renew their membership.

Key questions:

▶ *What area of restoration do you specialise in?*

▶ *Is the polishing/finishing technique you will be using on my antique true to how it would originally have been polished?*

CAR MECHANICS

In theory, if your car is experiencing any kind of problems, or if it just needs a general service, you should be able to take your car to any garage to have it repaired, providing you ask them beforehand that they will be able to definitely fix your car after describing the nature of the problem and the make and model of your vehicle. Some garages may not have the experience or capacity to repair very new cars or the wide range of green models that are now emerging (see box below).

If you do own a new car, bear in mind that some dealerships – the brand garages of the make of your car – are still propagating the myth that any car manufacturer's warranty you may have purchased will be invalidated if your car is serviced or repaired at any other garage. In fact, EU legislation was passed in October 2003, which ruled that cars can be repaired or serviced at any garage, as long as it is VAT-registered, without invalidating the manufacturer's warranty.

If you want to have a service done, check your owner's handbook to see what sort of service you will need – is it a 12,000-mile or a one-year service? Find out what will need to be changed, such as engine oil, oil filters, spark plugs and air filters, and what will need checking, such as the brakes, tyres, lights and suspension.

Where you take your car for repairs will depend on the problem you're encountering. If your car won't start, or it breaks down while you are actually driving it, you will be covered for the work if you're a member of the AA, RAC or equivalent breakdown service. You can also call out these bodies if you're not a member – they are likely to be cheaper than a garage. Bear in mind that some breakdown services won't come out to your house if your car won't start

Green gauges

If you own a hybrid technology car, Honda, Toyota and BMW recently worked with the motor industry to develop a qualification for car mechanics on maintaining green vehicles, under the Qualifications and Credit Framework (QCF).

Hybrid cars have a battery system that is central to the car's performance, unlike more conventional cars. The skills-based qualification, a Level 3 Award in Automotive Internal Combustion and Electric Hybrid System and Replacement, is offered to mechanics across the industry at the Honda Institute. A knowledge-based Level 2 qualification is now offered across the UK by colleges.

Rogue traders

A Which? investigation found that incompetent or dishonest mechanics are not a rare breed. Which? researchers took 50 cars for a service around the UK. The cars were checked beforehand by independent experts, who introduced five simple faults to each model. Afterwards, they checked the cars again to see if the faults had been rectified.

A high number of mechanics missed the faults, while some charged for unnecessary or non-existent work. A mere two of the 50 garages assessed gained full marks from inspectors for spotting all the faults and for their quality of work, while 46 garages missed at least one fault, and two missed all five.

Which? found no real difference in the work of franchised dealers and independent garages. But franchised dealers charge more for their work – some 35 per cent extra on average.

at home (unless your policy includes an 'at home service' clause) in which case you will need to call out your local garage at short notice.

If you own a new vehicle, check the terms of your manufacturer's warranty before embarking on any repair work – it could be invalidated if parts different from those stipulated in the warranty are used in any repair or service work.

Check to see if the car mechanic is a member of the Motor Industry Code of Practice www.motorindustrycodes.co.uk. At the very least, your car mechanic should hold an NVQ in car mechanics. Membership of a trade body or a local authority Assured Trader Scheme is also desirable. The Retail Motor Industry Federation (RMIF) and Bosch run quality schemes, which promise certain standards of quality.

The Retail Motor Industry Federation has an online directory of member firms which you can search at www.rmif.co.uk. This offers a complaints process if you're not happy with a member garage, which can help sort out any problems without needing to go to court.

In response to complaints about the garage industry, a new code of practice has been launched. The Motor Industry Code of Practice for Service and Repair went live in August 2008, and members of it will have to meet certain standards. The code is voluntary, so garages don't have to sign up to it, but it's hoped that many mechanics and garages will do so to prove they are committed to providing a good service and treating customers fairly. The Motor Industry Code of Practice for Service and Repair is currently working towards becoming an OFT-approved code.

All garages that subscribe to the Code have committed themselves to the following:

▶ Honest and fair services.
▶ Clear and transparent pricing.
▶ Doing work as agreed.
▶ Issuing invoices that will match the prices initially quoted.
▶ A straightforward complaints procedure.
▶ Competent staff.

The Code also has a free advice line for consumers and offers free conciliation and affordable arbitration.

Visit www.motorindustrycodes.co.uk for more information, or search for a garage near you that subscribes to the code at www.motorindustrycodes.co.uk/garagefinder.

Key questions:
▶ *What's your average response time?*
▶ *Are you VAT-registered?*
▶ *Are you a member of the Motor Industry Code of Practice?*

CHIMNEY SWEEPS

If your home has a chimney, it may need to be swept a number of times each year to prevent fires or carbon monoxide poisoning, which can arise from blockages. Your chimney needs a clear passage to allow dangerous combustion gases to exit your home. Cleaning will remove soot and creosote, and get rid of unwanted birds' or squirrel nests, rodents, cobwebs and other blockages.

If you are burning ordinary smokeless coal in your fire, a sweeping once a year by a professional sweep will be sufficient, rising to twice a year if you are burning domestic household coal. A chimney heated by a gas fire also needs sweeping once a year.

If you own a woodburning stove, which are becoming increasingly popular due to claims that burning wood is potentially carbon neutral, and the relative cheapness of wood in comparison with other fuels, your chimney needs to be cleaned seasonally. The National Association of Chimney Sweeps (NACS) advises that your chimney is cleaned three to four times a year, as wood generates more soot than other fuels.

Most chimney sweeps learn their craft on the job, although they may also have City and Guilds and NVQ qualifications in chimney engineering. Any sweep you are looking to hire should have been practising for at least two years.

All sweeps registered at the National Association of Chimney Sweeps (NACS) have qualified for membership through a practical assessment on site, and at the NACS Chimney Training Centre, and must hold professional indemnity insurance to join.

As of 2010, all workers in the construction sector, including sweeps, must hold a Construction Skills Certification Scheme (CSCS) card, or be registered in an affiliated scheme. To receive a card, traders must hold an NVQ or an acceptable equivalent, and pass a health and safety assessment. You can learn more at www.cscs.uk.com/smart-cards.

Key questions:
▶ *Are you a member of any trade association?*
▶ *How many years' experience do you have as a sweep, and where did you train?*

COMPUTER REPAIRERS

Personal computers now play a phenomenally large role in everyday life. Whether you work from home or pass your evenings chatting on Facebook, playing games or dealing with personal admin, the degree of reliance the majority of the British public has on this kind of technology means that when it fails, it can be devastating – especially if your data isn't backed up onto an external hard drive.

If your computer breaks down and is still under warranty, you can simply take it back to the place where you bought it and (if you have the original warranty and your receipt to hand) the store has a legal responsibility to sort out the problem, either by fixing it themselves or by sending it back to the manufacturer to repair. If it can't be repaired, you should receive a replacement computer. It is the shop's responsibility to do this, so don't be fobbed off if they say otherwise.

If your computer isn't under warranty, you can choose where you'd like it to be fixed. Look into whether an independent trader might be able to offer you a better service than the bigger companies; they're likely to be value for money and may come to your home to fix your machine.

Repair men and women may hold a National BTEC Award in computer engineering, the first UK nationally recognised qualification in computer assembly, repairs and maintenance, although some repairers may also hold degrees in computer science.

Check if they are a member of the professional body British Computer Society – you can search their online directory at http://wam.bcs.org.

You will also need to check before hiring how many years of experience they have and what type of computer this is in – a repairer with a lot of experience in PCs may not know how to repair an Apple Mac computer, for example.

Key questions:
‣ *Do you specialise in repairing PCs/Macs?*
‣ *How long will the repairs take?*

DRAINS SPECIALISTS

Healthy drains and pipes are the unsung heroes of the home, ridding it of every bit of water you use, from waste water to soil water from WCs and rainwater coming off the roof. But if they're not working properly, they can cause a number of problems, from nasty pongs to serious flooding.

Holiday hits
Drains are particularly prone to clogging over holiday periods such as Christmas, as they may not be able to cope with an increase in water usage or with the build-up of grease from Christmas roast dinners that you'll be throwing down the sink. It's a good idea to pour a kettle of boiling water down the drain once a week anyway to melt away any accumulated fat or grease, but be extra vigilant with this in busy periods. You can also collect any grease in a container and throw it straight into the bin.

Climate change

Given the extremes of rainfall we often see these days, if you're having an extension built, increasing your roof space or paving over your drive (for which you now need planning permission, see Section 1 for more details), you may also need to install a soakaway. A soakaway is basically a hole in the ground, which is filled with rubble or stone and then covered with soil, which must, in turn, have good drainage properties. Your local building control officer (BCO) will be able to provide advice on whether this is necessary.

Drains in most urban areas were built many years ago and are just unable to cope with increased rainfall. Flooding often occurs during periods of heavy rainfall because drains can't cope with the amount of water flowing into them.

Drainage is covered by the Building Regulations and if you are laying new drains, the work may need to be inspected by your local authority's BCO (see Section 1). You can download a copy of the current Building Regulations for free at www.planningportal.gov.uk.

Do-it-yourself drainage is often a bad idea. If your drains are clogged, any chemicals you use to unblock them yourself could actually be harmful to your pipes and cause internal damage. Equally, you may have a worse problem on your hands than you realise – for example, if tree roots, attracted by a build-up of moisture, have started to grow in your drains, this will cause blockages, which will most definitely need to be remedied by a professional.

If you have installed a washing machine, sink or toilet yourself, it's easy to plumb the appliance into the wrong part of the sewerage network. Wessex Water recently issued a warning that this could cause water pollution if appliances are draining into rainwater drains, rather than the sewerage system, resulting in dirty water being released into the watercourse.

All in all, it's best to hire a drains specialist or professional plumber (see Section 1) for repair work and to install your appliances. This will help avoid problems later down the line and prevent the cause of any unnecessary damage to your property that could be very expensive to fix.

The type of professional you hire to fix or lay new drains will depend on the nature of the job you need doing. If you're having new drains laid, builders and plumbers who are members of the Chartered Institute of Plumbing and Heating Engineering (CIPHE) can self-certify minor internal and external drainage work.

For clogged drains, you will need a plumber or drain engineer. If they are self-employed, they should have attained NVQ Level 3 in plumbing, or in construction for builders, and be a member of the CIPHE.

Key questions:
▶ *Are your trucks fully stocked or do you charge for going to get parts?*
▶ *Do you have experience in working with drains/plumbing in old/new properties?*

LOCKSMITHS

Planning to employ a locksmith will require a bit of thought as to what you actually want from the service beforehand. In cases where you're locked out of your house or need to change the locks urgently, this will be very clear. But you may also need to check that your security meets your insurance policy requirements, or want to improve the overall security of your home.

General services include the following:
▶ Helping you to get back into your home after a lock-out.
▶ Changing locks on cars and homes.
▶ Fitting new locks.
▶ Maintaining and repairing existing locks, including doors, windows and padlocks.
▶ Access control. Locksmiths may also fit security shutters, bars or grilles, fit safes or change combinations for safes if you've forgotten the code. Some locksmiths may also supply and fit CCTV and alarm systems, as well as performing a security survey to check how secure your home is, and highlight where upgrades will be necessary to meet the requirements laid out by your home insurance policy.

There are no nationally recognised qualifications such as NVQs for locksmithing, but the most recognised qualifications the industry accredits are those run by the British Locksmiths Institute (BLI), as well as the Auto Locksmiths Association (ALA). In Ireland, locksmiths may have taken exams run by the Associated Locksmiths of Ireland (ALOI).

If they are a member of the Master Locksmiths Association (MLA), your trader will have undergone criminal record checks and regular inspections to ensure the work they're producing is of good quality.

Key questions:
▸ *Will the locks you supply conform with British Standard safety marks?*
▸ *Is there a call-out charge?*

PIANO TUNERS

Despite the advent of the digital piano, its ancestor, the traditional acoustic instrument, remains massively popular, with thousands of pianos still gracing the living rooms of UK homes.

But they are sensitive creatures, susceptible to changes in humidity and temperature, and will go out of tune at least twice a year, even if they're never played. If it isn't tuned regularly, a piano's pitch will drop, rendering it virtually unplayable.

The piano's soundboard moves daily, shifting more abruptly with the seasons when winter and summer hit as the wood gets moist and swells, which pushes the bridge holding up the strings. Consequently, strings will go sharp in the summer and flat in the winter. A century ago, pianos were tuned four times a year, although now twice a year should be sufficient to keep your piano reasonably in tune, as they are manufactured to a higher standard than previously. Sadly, piano tuning is a dying art, and a shortage of piano tuners is looming on the horizon in the UK. Prices could be driven up significantly within the next five years.

Qualifications that piano tuners may hold vary between City and Guilds qualifications, HNDs or a degree in music technology. It's likely that most new tuners will hold a music technology degree, as there is only one college remaining in the UK that runs a formal qualification in piano tuning. On the job experience and training in shops and workshops also counts for a great deal in this field, as does membership of a trade body.

The Pianoforte Tuners Association (PTA) has a stringent admittance policy, in which members need to have been tuning pianos for seven years, or six if they have spent two years studying tuning at college. The PTA tests its tuners in three parts, with a practical tuning test, then two hours of standard repair work and, finally, a viva voce test, in which candidates can be asked anything about tuning. The PTA also runs yearly conventions in continuing personal development for members.

You can search the PTA's website at www.pianotuner.org.uk to find a PTA member within your postcode.

Key questions:
▸ *Where did you train?*
▸ *Are you a member of the trade association, the Pianoforte Tuners' Association (PTA)?*

REMOVAL FIRMS

Moving house is often quoted as being one of life's most stressful experiences, so it's unsurprising that many movers decide to hire a removal company to ease the process. Unless you are physically in top form and have a lot of friends who have committed to helping you move, going down the DIY method is often not worth it in terms of the stress it can generate for the money it will save you.

Removal companies can offer packages to any destination, whether you're moving within the UK or are relocating overseas. Some provide a full packing service for all your worldly goods, although if you're willing to do that yourself, all offer a more straightforward loading and unloading service.

The company you've shortlisted may have gained training through the British Association of Removers (BAR) or the National Guild of Removers and Storers. If not, then experience does play a major role in how effectively they will be able to do their job. Ask how many years they have been trading for and follow up any recommendations you receive with reference requests.

Key questions:
▸ *Will you charge extra for moving very large or difficult items?*
▸ *How many people will you supply to help the driver with the move, and what involvement will you require from me?*
▸ *Do you belong to the British Association of Removers (BAR)?*

What should you ask before hiring?
ANTIQUES RESTORERS

As usual, if you've had any good recommendations from family or friends, this is a helpful indicator of good service and practice in the antiques field. Shortlist two or three, and ask for former client references and for picture examples of former work.

Any restorer you hire should have a good academic approach to object restoration, along with a sound historical knowledge of a number of periods to keep the integrity of your piece alive. If you're unsure about your restorer, swot up on a period of furniture or painting history, and test them on it. If they falter, it's probably not a good idea to trust them with your possessions. Find out where they received their qualifications, and how long they have been practising their craft.

A good restorer should be able to distinguish between restoration and conservation. Restoration should aim to restore the object to its original form, but with a minimum of intrusion, and should mainly work to make it useable and attractive, again through sticking to its original design and construction. Bear in mind that excessive restoration will unfortunately degrade your object in value – many antiques dealers refuse to sell restored pieces on this basis, unless it is a piece of genuine historical value and has come from either a country house or a royal palace.

Conservation won't change the appearance of your object, as it deals with stopping deterioration, and preventing it in the future while not changing its original design or use. Show your object to your restorer, and ask them to examine it carefully, making sure they know what end result you'd like to achieve. They should then advise you on the mixture of conservation and restoration work you'll need to have done.

Take this opportunity to find out if your object is genuine. For example, a highly polished piece of furniture that you purchased believing it had eighteenth-century provenance, might date from a far more recent period. Your restorer will also be able to tell you if any scuff marks have been added to give your object an older appearance.

If your object has been altered in any way, your restorer will be able to advise on how it can be restored to its original form, determining what it was meant to look like originally, and what it should look like now.

If you're seeking advice on how to store your pieces (in the event of installing underfloor heating, for example) and you'd like to know how to protect your things from the change of environment, your restorer should be able to advise you on the best conditions in which your objects will be preserved. Placing any furniture, for example, in front of a radiator, is a rather bad idea, but if your home is rather cluttered or space is an issue, you could invest in a humidifier to combat the effects of central heating.

Trade body BAFRA publishes an *Antique Furniture Restoration and Conservation Guide* annually, in which it lists all its members, together with the specialist skills they hold, which costs £7.50. Alternatively, you can visit www.bafra.org.uk to access a full members list to find a restorer in your area.

CAR MECHANICS

It's difficult to distinguish the good garages from the bad ones. Personal recommendation is an invaluable pointer, so ask around to find a good verbal review. Which? Local also has a range of recommended traders in your area.

When you've drawn up a shortlist of suitable garages, call them with your details to ask them for quotes for the work you need doing. Note down who you've spoken to, and the price you've been given. Don't be too hasty to book your car in with the first garage you call – ringing round a few good garages, and playing them off against each other by quoting a cheaper service if it's been offered, could save you hundreds of pounds. Check if the quotes you've been given includes all parts, labour costs and VAT.

If you're having a service done, ask if the garage will stamp your service book, and if your car has a service warning or reminder light flashing, whether it will reset this after servicing. Check whether the garage will carry out the service in line with the manufacturer's procedures, using original parts for your vehicle, or those of an 'equivalent quality', which you will be able to establish by checking with your car manufacturer. This is crucial, as if you own a new vehicle, your car's manufacturer's warranty could be invalidated if, for example, the wrong part is fitted or the wrong type of oil is used when it is changed during the service.

When you've found the right garage for you, check when they can fit you in, and how long the work will take. Ensure they will check with you first before

I have taken my car to the garage because it's making a funny noise. They have said they will have a look at it, but it may take them a while to find out what it is. What are my rights?

Under the Supply of Goods and Services Act 1982, if a definite completion date or a price has not been fixed, then any work on your car must be completed within a 'reasonable time' and for a 'reasonable charge'.

In addition, any work must be carried out with 'reasonable care and skill' and materials used must be of a 'reasonable quality'. The garage can only charge for work that you have authorised.

If the garage doesn't meet any of the above conditions, it is in breach of contract.

▶ If the garage is taking too long to do work, you have the right to get another garage to finish the work and claim the extra cost back from the original company. However, you should notify the garage first of your dissatisfaction, giving it the chance to finish the work within a reasonable time.

▶ If the garage is charging too much, you have the right to only pay a 'reasonable sum' – this depends on how much work has been done on the car and the type of work undertaken. You will need to show this by evidence from other garages. If you find you are in dispute over a bill, you will need to look at whether you agreed a fixed price at the outset or relied upon an estimate. Generally, a quotation is a firm price and you should not have to pay any more than the initially agreed sum, whereas an estimate is only a provisional guide.

▶ If the work on your car is not of a satisfactory standard, then you may have a claim for defective workmanship. If you have lost confidence in the original garage's ability to do a good job, then you have the right to get another garage to fix the problem and claim the cost back from the original company. However, you should notify the garage first of your dissatisfaction. Alternatively, you can give the original garage the chance to remedy the defective work within a reasonable time before going elsewhere.

If you are forced to pay the garage a disputed amount in order to recover your car, make it clear in writing that you are paying under protest and without prejudice to any legal rights you may have against the garage.

Checklist

Before you ring any garages to arrange a service or repairs, arm yourself with the following information:

▶ Your car's model.
▶ Its age.
▶ Its mileage, engine size, fuel type and registration number.
▶ Any modifications that may have been made.

doing any work that might be required, or if something needs to be replaced that's not included in the service. Try to source a garage that is a member of the Motor Industry Code of Practice.

CHIMNEY SWEEPS

There is nothing like personal recommendation, so ask around before booking a sweep. When making the appointment, do check on how he/she keeps mess at bay; cleaning chimneys is, after all, a notoriously mucky job (see page 158).

COMPUTER REPAIRERS

Before you embark on any repairs, consider whether or not your machine is actually worth repairing. If you've had it for some years, it may be worth upgrading to a newer machine.

If you're convinced your computer is worth repairing, many manufacturers' websites list approved repairers. Check the make of your machine and log onto the manufacturer's website to see if this is an option. If you're looking to hire an independent repairer, ask around friends and family for recommendations, and check Which? Local for approved repairers in your area.

When you're shortlisting potential repairers, check that they will provide a 'no fix, no fee' service. Describe the problem over the phone, making sure you've noted down the make of your computer beforehand, and find out if the repair will be guaranteed.

Going up in smoke

Bear in mind that if your computer is still under warranty, and has been used in a smoking household, your warranty may be voided. In November 2009, American publication *The Consumerist* reported two cases from 2008 where Apple Mac refused to fix two computers that had voided their warranty. Apple stated that their reasons for voiding the warranties were the health risks of second-hand smoke for the repairers, and because the machines were contaminated with cigarette smoke they constituted a bio-hazard. Apple hasn't yet placed a clear disclaimer relating to second-hand smoke in its Apple Care terms and conditions, but you will need to check where you stand before sending your machine off for repair.

Don't always leap to take your computer into the big shops for repairs. Some stores have been found to overcharge for their services and misdiagnose basic problems - it's not unheard of for consumers to be advised to buy a new computer when all that's wrong with the machine is a missing file or loose wire.

Make sure you back up all of your data if you can before taking your computer in for repair, and delete anything that you wouldn't want somebody else to see. Don't risk your personal security by leaving personal data such as bank details on your machine.

Prices can vary massively for the same repair, so make sure you get a number of quotes from different shops before committing to anything.

DRAINS SPECIALISTS

When you've shortlisted a range of companies or traders, you should check that the firm in question has experience of working with your home's type of drain. If you own an older property, particularly if you're having your drainage extended, you will need a trader with experience of working with older drains, so it's a good idea to ask for examples of former work, and to amass two to three references from past clients.

If your WC, sinks or drains are blocked, check if your plumber or drain engineer will be bringing along a CCTV camera to detect the cause of the problem, as this may be necessary. If you are claiming for this kind of work on your home insurance, ask your insurance company to obtain at least three quotes for the work before committing to a particular company, to avoid higher than necessary premiums in the future.

Check how soon they will be able to come out to sort the problem – blocked drains should be unblocked as soon as possible, and the firm must have a good local network in your area to deal with your problem promptly. If you're having new drainage installed, ask for an estimate of how long the work will take.

You can also go through a trade association to find a suitable trader. The Chartered Institute of Plumbing and Heating Engineering (CIPHE) has around 12,000 members in the UK. You can find a drains specialist in your area at www.ciphe.org.uk and you can search the Association of Plumbing and Heating Contractors (AHPC) online directory at www.competentpersonsscheme.co.uk.

It is also a good idea to check with your council or water board that the drain causing the problem is your responsibility to fix – if you live in a row of terraces, it may not be. Your local authority may have diagrams of your drains, which they will charge you to have a look at.

Members of the Association of Plumbing and Heating Contractors (AHPC) are thoroughly vetted, and must have been trading for two years to join, carry at least £2 million in public liability insurance, meet the requirements of the Water Supply (Water Fittings) Regulation Approved Contractor Scheme and have a complaints handling procedure.

You can search for members of plumbing and drain-repair engineer trade bodies at the Institute of Plumbing at www.plumbers.uk.com and at the AHPC at www.competentpersonsscheme.co.uk.

LOCKSMITHS

Look to hire a locksmith with several years of experience. If you're hiring a relative newcomer to the trade, ask if they are licensed with the Master Locksmiths Association (MLA). You can check the MLA's website at www.locksmiths.co.uk, or call 0800 783 1498 if you're in any doubt. Check how many references they may have, and speak to people they've done work for previously. You can also check Which? Local to find recommendations for locksmiths in your area.

Check if your locksmith is a member of a legitimate trade association, ask for their membership details and call the association to confirm this. In turn, any association your trader is affiliated with should have accredited recognition and perform regular inspections of work.

Equally, the more information you can provide your locksmith with at the point of hiring, the better. Have you lost your keys or need to change the locks? What type of doors do you have? Check your home insurance to make sure your home security meets its requirements. If it doesn't, relay to the locksmith exactly what will need to be altered to bring your home security up to scratch.

If you're buying extra security products from your locksmith, check that these have been independently verified. Are they Sold Secure approved? Have they been tested in an independent house test, as recognised by insurers and the Association of Chief Police Officers (ACPO)?

You can look up products to check they have been approved at Sold Secure at www.soldsecure.com. Those that have been assessed and proven to be satisfactory will bear the Sold Secure Quality Mark. This is split into three categories: bronze, silver and gold, with gold being the highest indicator of the security provided by a particular product.

You can also visit the ACPO's Secured By Design website to search a directory of security products that have gained Police Preferred Specification status at www.securedbydesign.com.

Be wary of companies who advertise the fact that they don't charge call-out fees to draw in customers, only for the consumer to find out when they're on site that they have a minimum two hours labour charge. Some firms claim to only use non-destructive methods of entry if they're breaking into your home, even though in some cases, the quickest and cheapest way of re-entry may be by destroying the lock — don't fall foul of locksmiths who might be looking to charge you more by spending extra time to pick the lock unnecessarily.

PIANO TUNERS

A piano is an incredibly sophisticated instrument, made up of 5,000 parts. Establish your tuner has an intimate knowledge of pianos before letting them near what is likely to be one of your most prized possessions.

Consumers using a piano tuner generally enjoy a long relationship with their trader, as pianos need to be tuned at least every six months, so it's important to make sure they are up to scratch before hiring. Going on recommendations from family and friends is always a useful barometer of a tuner's ability, as is checking Which? Local for recommendations in your area. You can also visit the PTA's website to find a member in your area at www.pianotuner.org.uk.

It's vital to check where your tuner trained to learn his or her craft, whether this has been achieved in a shop (although this method of training is now redundant), or at college. If your trader can't provide this information, they're unlikely to have been trained properly, so don't hire them. The PTA has predicted a rise in rogue piano tuners as shortages of qualified tuners increase, thanks to the advent of the chromatic electronic piano tuner. A good tuner will tune your piano both manually, with a tuning fork, and with an electronic tuner. According to the PTA, the electronic version is not entirely reliable and will sometimes give out the wrong results. A tuner reliant on electronic kit is also

---

Caring for your piano

Like any piece of valuable furniture, your piano should be handled with care. Before getting a tuner in, you can minimise the work that may need to be done by following this short guide:

▶ Keep your piano clean, and never stand anything holding water on it, such as drinks or vases of flowers.

▶ Don't spray-polish your piano. If you own an older piano, clean it using a French polishing technique with a soft, clean cloth. If you own a newer model, it will only need to be wiped with a damp cloth and then gently dried.

▶ If you're having any building work done, drape your piano in protective coverings to protect it from a build-up of dust.

▶ Don't store it near windows, by the fire or in front of a radiator to protect it from rises and falls in humidity, which cause the soundboard to swell and detune the strings.

unlikely to be able to make any little repairs to your piano that are generally necessary during the tuning process, so check what equipment your tuner will be using before hiring.

A good tuner will also be able to advise on setting the correct height of your foot pedals, which may need adjusting, the height of the keys from the floor and buying accessories to enhance playing comfort, such as a piano lamp, a stool and a metronome if necessary.

Make sure your tuner has liability insurance before you hire them in case of injury or damage to your property. The area of your home most likely to suffer damage from the work is your carpet.

REMOVAL FIRMS

Going on recommendations from family and friends, and checking Which? Local for reviews of firms in your area, is always a good starting point. Find out how long the companies you've shortlisted have been trading for and whether you can contact their past clients for references.

Ask if the company is a member of a trade association. There are two recognised removal bodies, the British Association of Removers (BAR) and the National Guild of Removers and Storers. You can search for members in your area at www.bar.co.uk.

All BAR members have to abide by a code of practice that is approved by the Office of Fair Trading (OFT), which you can read at www.bar.co.uk. The National Guild of Removers and Storers enforces a compulsory membership on members

---

Are you insured?

Before hiring any company, the most important issue to establish is what level of insurance they will offer to protect your belongings, and to make sure that they have liability insurance in case a remover sustains an injury while moving your possessions. Where your things are concerned, is there an excess on the insurance? Check with your own household insurance policy if the amount you've been quoted by the company isn't enough, as you may already be covered.

Removals checklist

A good removal firm will also have questions to ask you before you move, so put together information on the following before contacting them:

▶ Where you are moving to.

▶ Your moving date, if you have one.

▶ How much furniture you are moving and how much is going into storage. This will help your removers to estimate the size of the truck they will need to send out.

▶ Your new address. The firm will want to plan out how many journeys will be necessary between your old and new homes.

▶ What access is like for moving furniture and parking.

▶ If the new owners of your home are moving in on the same day and if they will require access.

▶ The time that you will be getting the keys to your new home.

▶ Whether you need a full packing service or if you simply need your breakable objects packed.

to its Removals Industry Ombudsman scheme in the event of any complaints about the service you have received from the removers you've hired. Visit www.removalsombudsman.org.uk to learn more.

However, if you're looking to hire a smaller company that doesn't want to pay the memberships to either the Guild or the BAR, don't be put off – many family-run firms rely on word-of-mouth recommendations to gain work. Just ensure you get at least three references before hiring, and do a few small checks. For example, the company should have a full address to show you rather than just a PO Box number. If the telephone number you've been given is an 0800 number, remember that these can be easily transferred to non-traceable mobile numbers.

It's a good idea to meet a representative from your shortlisted firms before you commit to anything, and ask them to visit your home with the vehicle they'll be using for the move in tow as rogue traders have been known to buy stock pictures of flashy vehicles to put on their websites, which they have no intention of using.

Establish that the lorry or van they will be using is in good condition and will be clean as a new pin on moving day. Ask the company to visit you beforehand to go through any problems that could arise on moving day with access and unusually shaped or valuable objects.

Many removal companies are booked up weeks in advance, so when you're shortlisting companies, make sure they can fit in with your moving date. It's a good idea to give yourself at least three months to find the right firm, to ensure that you're not left with the last resort of entrusting your possessions to a company you don't really want to hire.

It's very important to sign a contract with removal firms, as it will lock the company into the dates and costs specified within, including the deposit you've put down. Check the terms and conditions before hiring. If the moving date changes, you may need to pay a cancellation fee to the company, which can sometimes be as much as 60 per cent of removal costs.

Make sure the date quoted on the contract is the same date you have agreed with the firm, as this crucial detail can often be missed. If certain items are being sent into storage, specify exactly what these are in the contract, and take similar precautions with any items that are being moved out of storage and into your new home.

Moving overseas?

If you are moving overseas from the UK, you may require a fuller service from your removers. Do you need a full pack service, where the removers will pack everything for you beforehand, or do you just need them to move the items you've already packed?

Note that a move overseas will require your goods to be packaged in export wrapping, which involves wrapping goods in paper blankets, corrugated paper and/ or cardboard to protect them. As a precaution, it's advisable to take out a marine insurance policy, which will cover your goods against damage, loss and theft. Move Me International Removals, who are members of the Financial Ombudsman Service, offers a marine insurance policy, which you can view at www.moveme.co.uk. Make sure you estimate exactly how much your goods are worth, as this could affect how much you can claim in the event of loss, damage or theft.

Some removers offer containerised storage, where your possessions are packed into wooden containers on the removal lorry, which are then forklifted off at the other end and placed into storage.

Note down any requests you have for certain objects to be protected and the agreement you've reached with the company on this – for example, they will wrap up your priceless Andy Warhol painting or handle your grand piano with extreme care.

Check in the contract if items packed by yourself and your family and not the removal company are covered in their insurance. Often, flat pack furniture isn't covered either.

What legal issues should you be aware of?

With miscellaneous trades, your best bet is to contact Trading Standards on 08454 04 05 06 or visit www.tradingstandards.gov.uk to check what sort of contract you may need to sign, or issues you will need to bear in mind, before hiring. Any form of contract you establish with them is likely to be verbal, but if a trader is a member of any genuine trade association, they will have a procedure in place if you need to make a complaint about the services you've received from one of its members.

However, Trading Standards recommends that to be certain of your rights, you should always get something in writing when commissioning any work, particularly if it's for a large amount of money. If you do this, check the terms and conditions the company is offering and go through the contract with a fine toothcomb, checking your rights to cancel the service, and whether doing this after a certain period of time will incur financial penalties, as with removal firms. If your trader hasn't included their terms and conditions in the contract, ask them to do so, and check before signing anything.

Details of costs, and the dates on which you've commissioned the work, should also be included in the contract. Make sure your trader has specified the exact amount you will be charged, including material costs and VAT, and put in writing that they will need to seek your permission to do any extra work that will go over the price you have been quoted.

Information about the trader's indemnity insurance should also be noted down in the contract – it's crucial to ensure you won't be liable for any injuries sustained to either traders or your property during the work. Ask to see evidence of this.

Bear in mind, too, that if the agreement to have work done was made within your home, you will have a cooling-off period of seven days in which you'll be able to cancel.

If the contract was entered into at a distance, whether you've done this by mail, email or fax, or over the phone or on the internet, you will similarly have a cooling-off period of seven working days.

You must inform your trader if you're cancelling the work in writing – by letter, email or fax. If you've put down a deposit, this should be refunded to you within a maximum of 30 days. If your trader doesn't inform you in writing that you're entitled to a cooling-off period, he or she is committing a criminal offence. Report them to your local Trading Standards.

More details on your consumer rights are available at www.businesslink.gov.uk and on pages 185–95.

COSTS AND TIMESCALES

R ates for employing miscellaneous trades often vary according to what part of the country you live in. If your home is in Kensington or Chelsea in London, you will be paying considerably more for the service, whereas if you live in Cornwall, for example, the rate is likely to be lower. If you live in London, or you're employing someone far from your home, you will need to factor in travel and parking costs. It is reasonable to expect to pay either the trader's congestion charge, which ranges between £8 and £10 depending on when the trader pays the charge, or reimburse them for their travel and parking costs.

Costs

ANTIQUES RESTORERS

Some restorers will charge a small fee for estimates on how much the job will cost and the work involved in the restoration of your furniture. This can be negotiated if you end up giving them the final job, and many companies making this charge offer to reimburse consumers the fee when they have been awarded the contract for the work.

Check beforehand exactly what you are paying for, and if you will need to reimburse your trader's travel costs if you are using a specialist in a different part of the country. Estimating approximate costs is difficult, as it will depend on the nature of the repair work you need to be done, and the level of time and skill involved. Repair costs can run to hundreds and potentially thousands of pounds, so before you engage anyone to do it, consider whether the costs of repair are higher than the value of your item(s). If you're having the work done to enhance value, it may not really be worth it in the long run.

CAR MECHANICS

Paying for services and repairs for your car is unavoidable, but paying over the odds for it isn't. In May 2008, Which? undercover researchers made 126 calls to independent garages and 182 calls to franchised garages across the UK to see how much it cost to service a number of different types of car.

The average price for a service is £141, based on calls Which? made across the UK to independent garages. The lowest price of £105 was found in Northern Ireland, while services in the south east and London were the most expensive at an average price of £171.

At a franchised garage, the average price for a service was £250. The highest priced car to service was a BMW 316 four-door saloon, which cost £350 on average, while the lowest price vehicle was the Vauxhall Astra (1.6), which has an average price of £169.

For services that are charged at hourly rates, the Which? team found that the average rate charged was £41 an hour at an independent garage. The lowest rate found was in Northern Ireland, which had a median price of £25 an hour, while East Anglia was the most expensive area with a median price of £56 an hour. The median hourly rate at franchised garages was £85 an hour. BMW garages charged the highest average price of £117 an hour for work, and Citroën and Peugeot garages charged the lowest median price of £76 an hour.

All prices quoted here include VAT for franchised garages, while the sums quoted for independent garages may not if they weren't VAT-registered. Check beforehand whether VAT is included in the total price, and ask them to estimate how much it will cost if it isn't.

When you come to pay, check that your bill gives an itemised list of the parts used and what was done to your car. You're entitled to see or take away any replaced parts, so ask if you're suspicious or unsure about any work that has been done.

Following repair work or a service, if your mechanic recommends some major repairs, make sure you ring around other garages to compare costs before giving the go-ahead to proceed.

If you see an environmental charge listed on your invoice, this relates to the use of oily rags, antifreeze, engine oil and tyres, which are all classed as toxic waste. The garage has to pay to dispose of these properly.

Members of the Motor Industry Code of Practice are committed to providing invoices that match quoted prices.

CHIMNEY SWEEPS

Sweeps tend not to charge an hourly rate for their work, but deal with each case, after you've described the work, on a fixed fee basis, excluding material parts and VAT.

If practical, it's worth asking your sweep to visit you before doing the work, as many carry binoculars and CCTV cameras with which to check out your chimney before going to work with their brushes. This will be necessary if you haven't had your chimney cleaned regularly, or have bought a new home and aren't sure when the chimney was last cleaned. If your sweep finds asbestos in your chimney or sees any loose bricks hanging down from the top of the chimney, a key indicator that something has gone structurally wrong, they are likely to seal off the area, put up a warning notice and advise you to hire a builder either to rebuild or reline your chimney.

Prices will vary again from region to region, depending on the cost of living in your area, with the highest price ranging between £80 and £90 if you live in central London, and the lowest at £40 in rural areas.

COMPUTER REPAIRERS

Prices to repair computers can vary significantly, so make sure you obtain a number of quotes from a few traders before you commit to any particular one. Ask if your quote includes labour, parts and VAT. When you've decided to employ a repairer, tell the shop you want them to ask for your permission before going ahead with any work over a certain price. If the repairer is coming to your home, check if they will factor in transport costs as part of their fee, and whether there is a sliding scale of charges that will rise depending on what time of day your computer needs fixing – weekends and evenings may be more expensive.

Find out if your repairer will also be adding a call-out charge to his or her fees, and whether they will bill you for collecting your machine to take it away and deliver it again when the job is done, if you're not taking it into a shop yourself.

Again, beware of hourly rates. It is very tempting for some repairers to drag out the work, and thus charge more for it than is necessary. If the repairer you have shortlisted for the job is charging for his or her work in this way, negotiate to see if a fixed fee for the job can be established.

DRAIN SPECIALISTS

As with any trade, the costs of hiring a drain specialist to fix or extend your drainage system will vary nationwide depending on the cost of living, and may fluctuate widely from region to region. You can protect yourself from unforeseen costs by going for a company with no call-out charge and no hourly rates to get rid of the plumber's temptation to drag out the job and charge more for it. Ask for a full estimate up front.

The Association of Plumbing and Heating Contractors (AHPC) insists that its members provide full written estimates and quotes to their customers, along with any material costs and VAT details that may be excluded from the fee, and stipulate the terms of payment for the consumer upfront.

LOCKSMITHS

Make sure you're aware of your locksmith's charging structure before hiring. Do they charge an hourly rate or a set fee? If they don't issue a call-out charge, is there a minimum labour charge? If they do issue a call-out charge, then what's included in it? Some locksmiths include the first 15 minutes they spend at your home in this charge, for example.

How much do they charge for labour and parts and is VAT added on top? Are there any cancellation charges if you need to cancel the work? This applies, for example, if you are locked out but then find a way in.

Locksmiths tend to charge on average £70, plus VAT, for work, depending on the nature of the job, although if it's just a simple lock-out door opening job, this may be less than £50.

PIANO TUNERS

Piano tuning is an affordable necessity for your piano, with most tuners offering a reasonable standard tuning fee. The Pianoforte Tuners' Association (PTA) recommends that additional pitch work should cost £15, while a standard tuning should cost on average £48 in the most expensive areas of the UK, and £36 in the cheapest, although in the Home Counties, most tuners will charge an average fee of £55. Few tuners charge an hourly rate for tuning, but for general repair work, a fee of £30 an hour plus materials is recommended. Most piano tuners don't qualify for VAT, but check before you hire your tuner whether parts will be included in your tuning, and whether the tuner will be charging for his or her travel costs.

Bear in mind that if you have made an appointment to have your piano tuned and miss it, some tuners will charge a missed appointment fee.

REMOVAL FIRMS

Rates and costs will vary across the country, but ensure you establish a fixed fee before hiring your firm, and avoid paying an hourly rate. It's a good idea to get a range of quotes before committing yourself, and also remember to compare the levels of insurance offered by each company.

Ask if the company will offer a discount if you're booking a slot outside of their peak operating times. It could be cheaper if you're moving from London at the weekend, when the congestion fee doesn't apply, or if you're moving on a weekday.

Some firms may also charge extra for moving very large or valuable objects, such as paintings or a piano.

Check your contract's terms and conditions to see what you will have to pay the firm if you cancel or change the moving date. If your remover cancels the job, the British Association of Removers (BAR) code of practice states that if a BAR-accredited mover cancels more than ten days before your agreed moving date, it must refund everything you have paid them in full, and refund you 150 per cent if they cancel less than ten days before the date you've set.

Timescales and schedules
ANTIQUE RESTORERS

The length of time that it takes to restore a piece of furniture depends on just how specialist a piece it is and whether remedial work needs doing, too. You might think that your sofa simply needs reupholstering, for example, but once a specialist takes a close look at it you might find the frame needs repairing, too. If it's a particular fabric you are looking to replace, lead times can be long.

CAR MECHANICS

The length of time taken to repair or service your vehicle will vary enormously according to the state your car arrived at the garage in, and what work needs to be done to repair or service it. If all you need is an oil change and a service, for example, this only takes a few minutes, and you could have your car back on the road very speedily. But if your car needs more intensive treatment, you could well find yourself without it for some time, until the garage has time to fix it, or has ordered in the parts they need. At the point of hiring a mechanic, it's therefore essential to find out how long you can expect to be without your car for, getting at least a ballpark idea, so you can make alternative transport arrangements if necessary.

Make sure you leave a contact number with your garage so they can reach you if they find something else wrong with your car, or discover something that needs replacing that's not included in the service.

CHIMNEY SWEEPS

Before your sweep arrives, you will need to have cleared a direct route to the chimney, making sure you've left enough room for them to work in. Remove any ornaments from the hearth and the mantelpiece, and clear your grate of any fuel, ash or rubbish to save the sweep from having to clean up before they start work.

The National Association of Chimney Sweeps (NACS) quotes an average job time of two hours for sweepings. This varies from chimney to chimney, taking longer if your sweep comes across rodents or a squirrel's or bird's nest, or if your chimney is particularly tall, but could take as little as 30 minutes if it's a straightforward sweep.

After your sweep has finished work on your chimney, ask their advice on how often the chimney should be swept in future. As previously mentioned, a good sweep will also be able to give advice on steps you can take to maintain your chimney in the future, such as installing a cap on top of your chimney, which would be inspected every year. The cap prevents animals and rubbish from entering the top of the chimney. However, it can deteriorate in bad weather, so the cap needs to be monitored annually to make sure that it is still in full working order.

I have just had my chimney swept and he left a terrible mess with soot and dust everywhere. As a result, my whole living room needs a thorough clean and the upholstery and curtains are ruined. What can I do?

Under The Supply of Goods and Services Act 1982 your chimney sweep should have carried out the work with reasonable skill and care. The fact that he has left your room in a mess would point to the fact that there has been a breach of the implied term to carry out the work with reasonable skill and care. As this constitutes a breach of contract claim, you could argue that you are entitled to damages arising as a result of the breach. In this case that would be the cost of cleaning the room if you employ a cleaner. If you clean the room yourself, you would not be able to recover any costs because you have not suffered a financial loss. Unfortunately, the courts would not allow recovery for inconvenience.

Regarding the upholstery and the curtains, you will need to have them checked to see whether professional cleaning will restore the items to how they were. If these items have been ruined and will need replacing, then the cost of doing this would be recoverable from your original chimney sweep. You would need to replace the items with similar quality and type curtain and upholstery fabric and finish.

Any repair work your chimney may need will probably require the sweep to come back another time if they can fix the problem, but caps can often be installed on the same day.

COMPUTER REPAIRS

Ask the shop or repairer to contact you immediately before they replace any software or hardware on your PC. If this is likely, ask them if you'll lose any data. Before taking your machine in, back up any valuable data, such as documents or photos, on a memory stick or an external drive, just in case your hard drive is damaged or erased.

How long your computer will take to fix will vary depending on the scale of the problem, but expecting to have your machine back in full working order within two days is reasonable. Ask for a time estimate on the phone or by email before you take your machine in to be fixed, and check that the shop or repairer doesn't have a huge backlog of customers to ensure that repairing your computer will be high up on their priority list.

DRAIN REPAIRS

Depending on the severity of your problem, a blocked or leaking drain or soil stack can be dealt with between one and three days. If you've experienced a series of blockages recently, it may be necessary to call in a plumber each year to clean your drains or snake your drain lines. Fitting new draining may take significantly longer – ask your trader to give you an estimate before hiring them.

If you are having new drainage installed, this may need to be inspected before it's covered by your local authority's building control officer, who will carry out an air or water test to make sure the drainage doesn't leak.

PIANO TUNERS

Most piano tuners give an estimated repair time for retuning and fine-tuning pianos of two hours, although the time taken could be far less, depending on how many tuning pins the tuner will need to adjust when he or she arrives and, of course, how bad a state the piano is in when you've called the tuner in. If you own a piano that's been made in the Far East by brands such as Yamaha or Kawai, tuning will take up to two hours as the tuning pins around which their strings are wrapped are set very tightly around a wooden block and won't necessarily move easily – during the tuning process, a tuner will need to move and adjust 90 per cent of the piano's pins.

Your tuner will be assessing your piano's health generally during tuning and may suggest small repairs, for example, if the wooden hammers that hit the strings have fallen off. Most such repairs will only take a few minutes and can be easily done at home.

REMOVAL FIRMS

Planning is key to a successful move. Before you go anywhere, draw up an inventory of your possessions to make sure that nothing is left behind.

Your move's logistics should have been outlined in your contract, but make sure you confirm when the van will arrive to collect your things, and what the estimated time is between loading up and finishing the job at both ends. Drawing up a room plan of your new home beforehand will also be gratefully received by the movers, as will making sure that each box is colour coded according to which room it's going into.

Ensure the directions you've provided to your new home are clear and accurate, and notify your removers of any parking or access issues at the other end. You should be able to pull off your move within a day, all being well.

4 MAKING A COMPLAINT

- Writing letters
- Your rights
- Taking your complaint to an ombudsman
- Trade associations and professional body complaints procedures
- Taking your complaint further

HOW TO COMPLAIN

Fingers crossed, if you've followed our guide to picking the right trader or professional to do your work, and by using a service that's been recommended by other customers on Which? Local, or by friends and family, you'll have received a good service. But if you're not happy with the work that's been done, there are a number of measures you can take to resolve the problem.

Trade associations and professional bodies advise that you try to resolve any disputes that may have arisen first with the trader or professional themselves, giving them a chance to put matters right before taking the matter further.

This is supported by the recent pre-action conduct practice direction introduced by the Civil Procedure Rules at www.justice.gov.uk, which actively encourages parties to settle the issues between them without the need to start proceedings (that is, a court claim). The principles that should govern the conduct of the parties are that, unless the circumstances make it inappropriate, before starting proceedings the parties should:

▶ Exchange sufficient information about the matter to allow them to understand each other's position and make informed decisions about settlement and how to proceed.

▶ Make appropriate attempts to resolve the matter.

Writing letters

Whatever service you've received, you should take up your complaint first in writing with the company responsible for the work, ideally initially targeting a person in authority. For example, in the case of professionals, if you're not happy with the work your accountant, architect, estate agent, financial adviser, solicitor or surveyor has done for you, you should complain to the business's senior partner, while in the case of trade jobs, you should take the matter up with the owner or chief executive of the business.

LETTERS OF COMPLAINT

Complain in writing as soon as you are aware of the problem; don't let your complaint go stale – it could affect your rights if you leave it too late before complaining.

When writing a letter, write 'complaint' clearly at the top of the letter and include any other important details, such as your policy, customer or account number. Word your letter clearly and politely so you are able to express the nature of your complaint properly and accurately. Make sure you've included your contact details, adding your name, telephone number and address to the letter. Also ensure you are sending it to the right address and the right person, keeping your letter brief, and including the following points:

▶ State the nature of the problem. Remember to stay calm. Don't let the emotion of the moment get to you.

▶ Evidence of the problem – photographs of poor workmanship, for example, copies of correspondence or receipts, a copy of the contract you signed if applicable. If asked to present these, send copies and keep the originals.

▶ If there is any legislation you can quote that will help your case, do so.

▶ Knowing your rights can help to resolve issues more quickly. Quote the relevant law, such as the Sale of Goods Act 1979 if you're complaining about faulty goods, or the Supply of Goods and Services Act 1982 if you get inadequate service.

▶ State that you'd like the company to remedy the problem and what action you would like them to take. What would it take to resolve your complaint – would you be satisfied with an apology, or do you want a repair, a replacement, a refund or compensation? Spell it out.

Be reasonable and fair in your request – don't ask for £2,000 in compensation if it will only cost £500 to fix the problem. Give them a reasonable timescale in which to respond and outline what this is in writing – 14 working days is ample time for a firm to respond, although the problem may take longer to resolve.

If you feel uncomfortable with writing the letter yourself, you can ask a friend or family member, or even the Citizens Advice Bureau, to help you – visit www.citizensadvice.org.uk.

It's a good idea to send your letter by special or recorded delivery so you have a record of whether the firm has received it, in case they plead ignorance of your letter when you've written or called to chase the matter.

If you don't hear anything by the deadline you've set the company, you may need to write again, so be prepared to be persistent. Keep a written record of the steps you've taken to complain, including dates and details of who you have addressed your complaint to.

FINAL LETTER BEFORE FURTHER ACTION

Your first letter may not have got the results you wanted, or you may have received no response to your complaint or query, in which case it's time to write a second and final letter in which you include the following:

▶ Restate the law or regulation of which the company is in breach, and clearly explain why.

▶ Don't allow yourself to be fobbed off – some of the common excuses include retailers saying you are too late to complain and should have done so within 30 days of purchase. In fact, you actually have up to six years to pursue a claim, and even if you have lost the right to reject the goods, you can still claim for repair or replacement.

▶ Another common excuse is 'we don't give refunds'. This is illegal – if something's faulty, you have a statutory right to reject it and get a full refund.

▶ Another is 'we don't guarantee products, go to the manufacturer' – do not be fooled by this, the contract is with the retailer.

▶ Or they may say 'we can't do anything without a receipt' – in fact, having a receipt is not a legal requirement, you just have to have evidence of when and where you bought the item in question, such as a credit card statement or a cheque stub.

▶ A sentence stating that unless the company deals with your complaint properly and promptly, you'll take further action. This may be in the Small Claims Court or going to an ombudsman or trade or professional association, depending on the problem.

If you fail to come to an arrangement with the company involved, it's time to contact their trade or professional association, or to take the matter to Trading Standards or Consumer Direct (see page 178) if they aren't a member of any such body. You may also need to consult a solicitor if your complaint is complex or involves a large amount of money.

It may even be worth checking your household insurance to see whether you have the benefit of any legal expenses insurance, which may take on your case.

Your rights

Being aware of your rights as a consumer will also put you in a position of power when challenging work that has been badly done. The law states that you are entitled to the following:

▶ To receive work of a reasonable standard and quality.
▶ To have the work carried out within a reasonable timeframe.
▶ Receive the specific services that have been agreed between you and the professional or trader, whether in writing or verbally.

THE SUPPLY OF GOODS AND SERVICES ACT 1982

The main law covering services is the Supply of Goods and Services Act 1982. This covers the work done, or products supplied by, traders and professionals. If you've paid anyone to provide a service for you, this Act applies to them. Under the act:

▶ Work should be done using 'reasonable care and skill' to a standard you'd expect from a qualified and experienced trader or professional.
▶ Work should be done with materials of 'satisfactory quality', which are 'fit for their purpose'. Any goods supplied are also covered under this clause.
▶ Goods supplied must be 'as described'. For example, if you've had a new bathroom fitted, your shower must not only work, it must be the make and model you originally requested.
▶ Work should be done in a reasonable timeframe, unless you've agreed on a specific time or had to delay work for any reason, which should have been put in writing at the time.

SECTION 75 OF THE CONSUMER CREDIT ACT 1974

If you have paid for a service using your credit card, you are entitled to receive your money back under the terms of Section 75 of the Consumer Credit Act 1974 if necessary, if the firm you've used has gone bust, or you can't get a response from them to resolve your problem. Your credit card provider is responsible, along with the trader concerned, for any breach of contract, or misrepresentation and you will be able to claim back your deposit and other expenses you may have incurred for goods and services costing between £100 and £30,000. You don't have to have paid for all the work on your card, as even a small deposit will make your card provider liable, and then you will be able to get enough cash together to pay someone else to do or complete the work.

Phone your credit card company and say you want to make a Section 75 claim, requesting a claim form.

You could also get back some of the cash you've paid out if you used a Visa debit card, under the Visa Debit Chargeback system, but you'll need to contact your bank immediately to make sure you're covered to make a claim. Ask to speak to a supervisor at your bank if your claim is being blocked – some staff may not be aware of this protection. Chargeback isn't enshrined in law, unlike Section 75 – but the Financial Ombudsman Service (FOS) has deemed that allowing chargeback is 'good practice' as it is widely accepted by the banking industry.

UNFAIR CONTRACT TERMS AND EXCLUSION CLAUSES

Before you signed on the dotted line of any contract you may have drawn up with your trader or professional, you should have read all the small print, as both you and your trader or professional are legally bound to follow what's in it. However, any clause seeking to exclude or restrict your rights faces a number of obstacles. One is a question of interpretation; that is to say, the courts have always taken the view that an exclusion clause is to be construed strictly, so that any ambiguity is resolved against the party seeking to rely on the clause.

More important in recent times has been the statutory control imposed on exclusion and limitation clauses under the Unfair Contract Terms Act 1977 and the Unfair Terms in Consumer Contracts Regulations 1999.

The 1977 Act made it impossible for any contract term to exclude or limit liability for negligence that resulted in death or personal injury. It also rendered automatically void any contract term that sought to limit or exclude the implied terms as to description, fitness for purpose and satisfactory quality.

The 1999 Regulations go much further than the 1977 Act, with which it often overlaps. The Regulations provides protection against any unfair terms or clauses that create a significant imbalance in the contractual relationship to the detriment of the consumer – any clauses that are biased towards the company or try to take away your legal rights. This also protects you from any written terms that haven't been expressed in plain, intelligible language. If there's any doubt about the meaning of any term, the interpretation most favourable to you as the consumer will be assumed to be correct. The Regulations do not apply to the contract description or to the price or charge, so long as these are expressed in plain, intelligible language.

If, when reading through your contract again, you come across a term that is unfair, report it to the Office of Fair Trading, with a copy of the contract enclosed. Visit www.oft.gov.uk/, for more information, and Consumer Direct's unfair contracts section at www.consumerdirect.gov.uk to find out if you'll be able to take further action.

Taking your complaint to an ombudsman

An ombudsman acts as an independent judge to deal with any complaints you might not have been able to resolve yourself. It investigates both sides of the story to come up with a solution that is fair. Usually, traders or professionals must be members of an ombudsman scheme to allow you to be able to use it.

Before you contact any ombudsman service, you will need to check the conditions of each scheme – they may have time or compensation limits. Once the ombudsman has investigated the complaint, they will recommend the company you've taken action against do one or some of the following:

▶ Explain why they treated you in the way they did.
▶ Apologise.
▶ Change their practices or procedures to make sure what happened to you doesn't happen to their future clients.
▶ Pay you compensation.

Here are the ombudsman schemes that may be relevant to your complaints.

FINANCIAL OMBUDSMAN SCHEME (FOS)

This addresses any complaints you may have about banks and other financial advisers. They legally have up to eight weeks to investigate your complaint, but if you're unhappy with the response you have received, you can ask the FOS to step in. The FOS's free dispute-resolution service is designed for consumers to use without the need to get legal representation. You can fill in a complaints form at www.financial-ombudsman.org.uk or call the FOS on 0845 080 1800 or 0300 123 9 123 to get help with the complaints form over the phone.

You should print this off and send it to the FOS by post, along with any other documents that may be relevant to your complaint, and wait to hear from them to see if they can help you. The FOS can order firms and banks to resolve your complaint, including ordering compensation of up to £100,000.

If you live on the Isle of Man and have a complaint, you will need to take it up with the Isle of Man Financial Services Ombudsman Scheme at www.gov.im/oft/ombudsman, or if you live in Ireland, you'll need to visit www.financialombudsman.ie.

OFFICE OF THE LEGAL SERVICES OMBUDSMAN (OLSO)

The Office of the Legal Services Ombudsman (OLSO) can handle complaints against solicitors, barristers, licensed conveyancers and legal executives in England and Wales. You must write to the OLSO within three months of receiving a final decision letter from your solicitor, providing the following if you're not happy with the way your complaint has been handled:
▶ Clearly state in writing the reasons why you're unhappy with the way your complaint has been handled, or with the decision that the firm has reached.
▶ The firm's reference number and the name of the lawyer at the firm.
▶ A copy of the final decision letter you've received.
You can fill in a complaint form online at www.olso.org or call 0845 601 0794 to request a paper copy of the form. The OLSO should deal with your complaint within six months unless it is particularly complex. It has the power to recommend that you receive compensation or that the firm reconsiders their decision.

Visit www.olso.org for more information.

THE PROPERTY OMBUDSMAN (TPO)

The Property Ombudsman (TPO), formerly the Ombudsman for Estate Agents (OEA), can receive complaints about estate agents, letting agents, surveyors who are members of the RICS, and chains owned by banks, building societies and insurance companies within 12 months of the event, although it doesn't cover disputes over property surveys. You can use the TPO's services to make a complaint if you believe your legal rights have been infringed, if agents haven't followed the TPO's code of practice or if they have treated you unfairly or lost you money or caused you stress through inefficiency.

It is mandatory for all estate agents to belong to an ombudsman scheme, so you can be confident that your complaint will be dealt with if necessary. Bear in mind that the TPO won't review a complaint until you have gone through the firm's internal complaints procedure, and you have to give them eight weeks to solve your complaint. Visit www.tpos.co.uk for more information.

Many ombudsman schemes' decisions are legally binding and the company has to abide by their decision. Most firms tend to do what their ombudsman recommends anyway, for fear of being thrown out of the scheme.

Bear in mind that an ombudsman's decision is final, and you may not be able to appeal if you don't agree with it. If you are still not happy, you can take your case to court.

REMOVALS INDUSTRY OMBUDSMAN SCHEME (RIOS)

The RIOS has been set up to resolve disputes between consumers and companies they may have encountered a problem with, although you can't contact them unless you have failed to receive a satisfactory outcome from the firm you have a complaint with. It will investigate your complaints for free, including breaches of its code of practice – see www.ngrs.co.uk for details – and all members of the National Guild of Removers and Storers (NGRS) are covered in the scheme.

If you don't have enough evidence collated to support your claim, it may be overruled. The RIOS won't investigate complaints about insurance, or complaints which have already been dealt with by a court or another trade body. Visit www.removalsombudsman.org.uk for more information or to download a complaints form.

SURVEYORS OMBUDSMAN SERVICE (SOS)

The Surveyors Ombudsman Service (SOS) exists to deal with complaints made against chartered surveying firms that are members of the Royal Institution of Chartered Surveyors (RICS). It can also now help with complaints against estate agents. Again, this service is free, but action will only be taken if one of the ombudsman's members is involved.

To submit a complaint, you must have told the firm involved about the problem within 12 months of realising it and already have lodged a complaint through its internal complaints procedure.

The SOS allows firms up to eight weeks to sort out the problem. If you receive what they call a 'deadlock letter' from the firm saying they can't resolve your complaint, you have six months to pass it on to the ombudsman. You can call the ombudsman on 0330 440 1634 or 01925 530 270 to register a complaint, or visit www.surveyors-ombudsman.org.uk for more information.

Trade associations and professional body complaint procedures

Most trade associations and professional bodies have comprehensive and thorough complaints procedures in place. The mere mention of getting one involved is often enough to get your trader or professional to resolve your complaint quickly, as members tend to prize their membership highly.

We've listed the main trade associations and professional bodies for the trades mentioned in this book overleaf with details of their complaints procedures. You may also wish to visit www.taforum.org where you can search the trade association you are looking for by:

▶ Name.
▶ Activity.
▶ Initial letter.

When lodging a complaint, ask detailed questions about how the association's complaints procedure works. Find out how long disputes are likely to take to be resolved, and ask them if they think it's worth pursuing if the outcome will be in your favour.

BUILDERS AND CONTRACTORS

Arboricultural Association (AA): The AA requests that complaints about member tree surgeons be put in writing and sent to its head of support services (see Contacts and links, page 185). Your complaint won't be processed if it's made over the phone. Unless your tree surgeon has behaved in a manner the AA considers to be unethical or unprofessional, your complaint won't be processed. The AA doesn't issue consumers with any compensation.

If your complaint is found to be valid, the AA's complaints panel will review your case and invite both parties to submit evidence within 14 days. If your complaint is successful, the AA will either reprimand the trader, potentially naming and shaming them in the AA newsletter and, if necessary, terminate their AA membership.

Federation of Master Builders (FMB): The FMB runs an arbitration and mediation service for traders and consumers for its members. It will take four weeks from the date of your complaint application in order to determine the outcome of the dispute, and costs both you and the trader a non-refundable £200 each, plus VAT. A cheque made out to the FMB should be submitted with your application form.

You can get more information on the service and print off an application form at www.idrs.ltd.uk.

TrustMark: If you hired a trader who is a member of the TrustMark scheme, you can lodge a complaint with them if the trader hasn't come up with a suitable solution. TrustMark will investigate if the trader acted correctly, although it won't investigate the issue your complaint was actually about or give out any compensation. You need to have complained first to the trader and then to the scheme operator before you can contact TrustMark with a complaint.

If TrustMark finds that the trader didn't act correctly, they should ask them to look at your complaint again or remove them from the scheme altogether. You can't hire anyone else to sort out the work for you while your complaint's being looked at as TrustMark give firms a chance to complete the work or fix any defects. If you do hire another trader or contractor, the trader will be entitled to end the complaints process.

Some trade associations and bodies are now TrustMark members. These include the following:

- Association of Professional Landscapers (APL)
- Electrical Contractors' Association (ECA)
- European Fencing Industry Association (EFIA)
- Glass and Glazing Federation (GGF)
- Kitchen Bathroom Bedroom Specialists Association (KBSA)
- National Federation of Roofing Contractors (NFRC)
- Windows and double glazing body Fenestration Self-Assessment Scheme (FENSA).

You can download a form outlining the TrustMark complaints procedure at www.trustmark.org.uk or contact them on 01344 630 804.

PROFESSIONALS

For accountants: If you have a complaint about an accountant who is a member of the Institute of Chartered Accountants in England and Wales (ICAEW), you can contact the ICAEW after you have written a letter to the practice's senior partner outlining the problem.

If you have a complaint about investment business work, insolvency practice or audit work, visit /www.icaew.com and click on Protecting the Public, where you can also download a complaints form.

If the ICAEW feels it is a disciplinary matter, they will either give the accountant a chance to resolve the complaint through conciliation, or decide to investigate. If it's a non-disciplinary complaint, the ICAEW offers mediation and arbitration for both parties.

Visit www.accaglobal.com to find out the route to take if your firm is a member of the Association of Chartered Certified Accountants (ACCA).

For architects: Complaints against architects should be taken to the Architect's Registration Board (ARB). Your complaint must be in writing, and will only be dealt with if the architect has fallen below the standards set out in the ARB's code of conduct. Compensation for bad service won't be awarded.

After receiving your complaint, the ARB will pass it on to its investigations committee, where it will either dismiss the complaint, give the architect a formal written warning, or refer the complaint to the ARB's professional conduct committee for a public hearing. This process will take 12 weeks, although the complaint in total could take months to resolve, especially if it's a complex case.

Visit www.arb.org.uk for more information, or download the online complaints form at www.arb.org.uk.

For estate agents: If the estate agent is a member of the National Association of Estate Agents (NAEA), then you can take your complaint to the association. Investigations follow the procedures outlined in the NAEA's disciplinary procedure regulations. For more information, see www.naea.co.uk. See also The Property Ombudsman and Surveyors Ombudsman Service on pages 172–3.

For financial advisers: The place to turn to for furthering complaints against financial advisers is the Financial Ombudsman Scheme (see page 171).

For solicitors: If you want to complain about your solicitor's conduct or work, you should go to the Solicitors Regulation Authority (SRA). The SRA works alongside the Legal Complaints Service, which will become the Office of Legal Counsel (OLC) in 2010. The service is free and can help if you have any of these complaints about your solicitor if they have:

▶ Not done what you instructed them to do.
▶ Caused unreasonable delays, such as in the case of a property purchase.
▶ Given you inaccurate or incomplete information.
▶ Not kept you informed throughout the case on its progress.
▶ Given you the wrong information on how much you'll be charged for the work.

You can call the Legal Complaints Service helpline on 0845 608 656, or download a complaints form at www.legalcomplaints.org.uk. Your complaint should be resolved within six months. See also the Office of the Legal Services Ombudsman (OLSO) on page 171.

For surveyors: If your surveyor is a member of the Royal Institute of Chartered Surveyors (RICS), you will be able to complain about the service you have received and if you're not happy with the conduct of your surveyor. The RICS introduced a mandatory complaints handling procedure (CHP) for members in 1998, under which firms must appoint someone to handle your complaint and carry out an investigation. The RICS recommends mediation if you are unhappy with the outcome. Visit www.rics.org to download a guide on the RICS complaints procedure.

The RICS doesn't look at issues of professional competence and isn't able to give financial compensation. See also the Surveyors Ombudsman Service on page 172.

MISCELLANEOUS TRADES

For antiques restorers: If you have hired a restorer who isn't a British Antique Furniture Restorers' Association (BAFRA) member and something has gone horribly wrong with a restoration job, ask a BAFRA member to look at the work done and write a report as an expert witness before taking the case to court. Before you decide if it is worth it, balance up the costs of taking the case to court and the charges of the BAFRA member to appear as an expert witness against the money you need to recover from the restorer.

You can search for BAFRA members online at www.bafra.org.uk. For issues with BAFRA members, you can fill in an enquiry form at www.bafra.org.uk.

For car mechanics: See the Trading Standards and Consumer Direct panel, overleaf.

For chimney sweeps: The National Association of Chimney Sweeps (NACS) has a strict complaints procedure if you are unhappy with any aspect of your sweep's work or conduct. Call 01785 811732 to request a complaints form and the NACS will investigate.

For computer repairers: See the Trading Standards and Consumer Direct panel, overleaf.

For drains specialists: See the Trading Standards and Consumer Direct panel, overleaf.

For locksmiths: See the Trading Standards and Consumer Direct panel, overleaf.

Trading Standards and Consumer Direct

For all trades that aren't represented by a particular association or guild, your best option before going to court is to report the matter to the Trading Standards Institute (TSI) or to Consumer Direct.

Trading Standards runs an accredited trader scheme called Buy With Confidence, online at www.buywithconfidence.gov.uk. If your trader fails to resolve your complaint, they may be taken off the scheme, which is something most traders are keen to avoid.

Consumer Direct has detailed a comprehensive complaints procedure method on its website at www.consumerdirect.gov.uk, or you can call Consumer Direct on 08454 04 05 06 if you have any further questions.

Piano tuners: The Pianoforte Tuners' Association (PTA) doesn't get involved in resolving disputes with tuners, but it's important to let them know in writing if you have a complaint against one of their members and also let them know the outcome. If the issue is serious enough, they may suspend the membership of the tuner involved.

Removal firms: All members of the National Guild of Removers and Storers (NGRS) are members of the Removals Industry Ombudsman Scheme (RIOS, see page 172). The British Association of Restorers (BAR) offers a dispute and conciliation service between its members and their customers. Call the BAR on 01923 699480 to request a complaints form.

Taking your complaint further
ARBITRATION

In arbitration, two parties in dispute – in your case, you as the consumer and your trader or professional – ask an independent arbitrator to come up with a decision to solve the dispute. The arbitrator will look at evidence from both sides. There may then be an informal hearing where both sides can present their cases.

Arbitration decisions, which are known as the 'award', are legally binding for both parties. The arbitrator's decision is final, so you will only be able to take the matter to court afterwards in exceptional circumstances. A decision could take the format of, for example, paying compensation or forcing your trader to redo work that's been done badly.

It's worth checking with trade or professional associations if they have arbitration schemes for disputes – the Federation of Master Builders (FMB) is one that does, for example.

If you'd like to use arbitration but there is no industry scheme for you to fall back on, you can use a private arbitration service. You can search the Chartered Institute of Arbitrators' members directory online at www.ciarb.org.

GOING TO COURT

Taking your complaint to court should be your last resort, and only undertaken if you have tried all the complaints procedures that we have listed above and failed. Traders and professionals will have their insurance, and may have the backing of their association, so their legal expenses will be covered – unlike yours, which will come out of your own pocket, unless of course you have the benefit of any legal expenses insurance on your household policy.

It can take a few months between starting your claim and getting a judgement on whether you will be receiving your money back. Fortunately, sometimes the mere threat of court action is enough to persuade your trader or professional to settle, so ensure you give them a chance to act before you begin your claim.

EVALUATING THE CASE

If you are left with no alternative but to start court proceedings you must first ask yourself three basic questions:
▶ Do I have a good chance of winning?
▶ If I win, will I be able to recover the money from the other side?
▶ Is the amount at stake worth the cost of the court case?

THE SMALL CLAIMS COURT

Taking your case to the small claims section of the County Court is a fairly quick and simple method of sorting out a dispute. Remember always to be mindful of the Pre-action Conduct Practice Direction, the aim of which is to settle the issue between the two parties without the need to start proceedings. You can view it online at www.justice.gov.uk.

Small claims costs in England and Wales
Starting a claim: The fees to issue the proceedings are as follows (the www. moneyclaim.gov.uk online fees are in brackets). Where the sum claimed:
▶ Does not exceed £300 – fee £30 (£25)
▶ Exceeds £300 but does not exceed £500 – fee £45 (£35)
▶ Exceeds £500 but does not exceed £1000 – fee £65 (£60)
▶ Exceeds £1000 but does not exceed £1500 – fee £75 (£70)
▶ Exceeds £1500 but does not exceed £3000 – fee £85 (£80)
▶ Exceeds £3000 but does not exceed £5000 – fee £108 (£100)
▶ Allocation questionnaire: £35 if your claim is between £1,500 and £5,000
▶ Hearing fee: £25–£300, depending on the size of the claim

Small claims costs in Northern Ireland
Starting a claim: this is dependent on the size of your claim. If it doesn't exceed £300, it is £30; £50 if not over £500; £70 if over £500 and under £1,000; and £100 if over £1,000 and under £2,000.

Small claims costs in Scotland
Starting a claim: £45 for claims up to £3,000.

You may also incur other costs during your claim. These may include travel, accommodation and loss of earnings expenses for witnesses. The losing party must pay the winning party's costs, where reasonable.

Letter before action

Before commencing any action in the County Court it is necessary to write to the trader (the proposed defendant) advising him/her of your intention to take action via the small claims section of the County Court. Your letter should include:

▶ The nature of complaint.
▶ Details of how you want the matter resolved.
▶ A time limit for a response: seven or 14 days.
▶ An indication of intention to pursue a claim in County Court.

You should keep a copy of the letter together with proof of postage. This often produces the money you're owed, and quickly, while you may also be penalised by the courts on costs if one hasn't been sent.

You won't need to pay for a solicitor to act for you, and the hearing is informal. In England and Wales, there is a monies claims limit of £5,000, while in Scotland it is £3,000 and in Northern Ireland £2,000.

You can start your claim online at www.moneyclaim.gov.uk, or by going to your local court to pick up the relevant forms to fill in. Most court offices are open between 10am and 4pm. You will be able to find your court's address and phone number in the phone book or the Yellow Pages, under Courts, or on the HM Courts website at www.hmcourts-service.gov.uk.

Before starting a claim, consider whether the firm will be able to pay the amount you are looking to recover. If the firm is bankrupt or has gone into administration, this may be unlikely. First check whether the firm you're claiming from is still in business at Companies House at www.companieshouse.gov. uk, or by contacting the Insolvency Service on 020 7637 1110. You will need to have the full name of the company to hand and their latest address, and the Insolvency Service will be able to tell you if the company is in 'compulsory liquidation' – whether they have stopped trading.

There is a fee to start a small claim, and you won't recover your legal costs.

Once you've made a claim, the court will issue the trader or professional with a letter, giving them seven days to pay you – in Northern Ireland, this is 14 days. If you receive payment before the matter goes to court, you will need to pay a processing fee of £25. If you receive nothing, you can go ahead with issuing the proceedings.

THE COUNTY COURT

If you are claiming for more than £5,000, but less than £25,000, you can apply for a Fast Track procedure. If you're owed more than £25,000, you will need to apply for a Multi-Track.

Before you start looking for a solicitor to advise you on how successful your claim is likely to be, check that the trader you are claiming against actually has the money or assets to pay you if you win. You can assure yourself of their financial stability by visiting Companies House or calling the Insolvency Service, as outlined above.

It is then worth looking for a solicitor who offers to take on your case on a 'no win, no fee' process – although if you lose, you may have to pay the costs of the other party, which are likely to be significant.

Visit www.hmcourts-service.gov.uk for more information on the process.

MEDIATION

Mediation is a much cheaper way to resolve a dispute of this size. Costs outlined by the National Mediation Helpline state that the service, dependent on the amount you're claiming for, will cost £300 an hour plus VAT for a three-hour session if you're owed between £5,000 and £15,000, or £425 an hour plus VAT for a four-hour session if you're claiming between £25,000 and £50,000.

If your claim is for more than £50,000, you'll need to agree fees directly with the firm providing the mediation. Visit www.nationalmediationhelpline.com for more information.

THE HIGH COURT

If you are claiming for over £50,000, your case will be heard in the High Court. If your dispute is building-related, it will be heard in a specialist section of the High Court, known as the Technology and Construction Court (TCC), where all judges are experts in the construction field. For more information, visit www.hmcourts-service.gov.uk.

NOT BEEN PAID YET?

If your claim has been successful, but your trader hasn't yet coughed up the monies owed, a number of enforcement measures can be used to make sure they pay you, which include:

▶ An attachment of earnings order. If your trader works for a company, you will be able to deduct money from their wages directly, but you won't if they're self-employed.

▶ A warrant of execution. This authorises bailiffs to enter your trader's property and take goods to the value of your claim to sell at auction. This is a pretty extreme measure and should only be considered as a last resort.

▶ An oral examination. Your trader will need to come into court to be questioned by a judge, although this is voluntary in the first stage. If the trader refuses, you can apply for a court order to force them to do so. If they refuse again, they will be in contempt of court and liable for a term in prison.

Contacts and links

BUILDERS AND CONTRACTORS

The Arboricultural Association
Ullenwood Court
Ullenwood
Cheltenham
Gloucestershire
GL53 9QS
Tel: 01242 522152
www.trees.org.uk

The Association of British Insurers
51 Gresham Street
London
EC2V 7HQ
Tel: 020 7600 3333
www.abi.org.uk

The Association of Heating and
Plumbing Contractors (AHPC, England
and Wales)
12 The Pavilions
Cranmore Drive
Solihull
B90 4SB
Tel: 0121 711 5030
www.competentpersonsscheme.co.uk

The Association of Professional
Landscapers (APL)
Horticulture House
19 High Street,
Theale, Reading,
Berkshire
RG7 5AH
Tel: 0118 930 3132
www.landscaper.org.uk

Construction Employers Federation
143 Malone Road
Belfast
BT9 6SU
Tel: 028 9087 7143
www.cefni.co.uk

Energy Saving Trust
21 Dartmouth Street
London
SW1H 9BP
Tel: 020 7222 0101
www.energysavingtrust.org.uk

Federation of Master Builders
Gordon Fisher House
14-15 Great James Street
London
WC1N 3DP
Tel: 020 7242 7583
www.fmb.org.uk

Federation of Plastering and Drywall
Contractors (FPDC)
1st Floor
8/9 Ludgate Square
London
EC4M 7AS
Tel: 020 7634 9480
www.fpdc.org

Flooring Industry Training Association
(FITA)
4c St. Mary's Place
The Lace Market
Nottingham
NG1 1PH
Tel: 0115 950 6836
Fax: 0115 941 2238

Gas Safe Register
PO Box 6804
Basingstoke
RG24 4NB
Tel: 0800 408 5500
www.gassaferegister.co.uk

Glass and Glazing Federation
44-48 Borough High Street
London
SE1 1XB
Tel: 0870 042 4255
www.ggf.org.uk

Guild of Builders and Contractors
Crest House
102-104 Church Road
Teddington
Middlesex
T211 8PY
Tel: 020 8977 1105
www.buildersguild.co.uk

Institute of Carpenters
3rd Floor D
Carpenters' Hall
1 Throgmorton Avenue
London
EC2N 2BY
Tel: 0207 256 2700
www.instituteofcarpenters.com

Joints Contracts Tribunal
4th Floor
28 Ely Place
London
EC1N 6TD
Tel: 020 7637 8670
www.jctltd.co.uk

Kitchen Bathroom Bedroom Specialists
Association
Unit L4A
Mill 3
Pleasley Vale Business Park
Mansfield
Notts
NG19 8RL
Tel: 01623 818808
www.kbsa.org.uk

National Federation of Builders
55 Tufton Street
London
SW1P 3QL
Tel: 08450 578 160
www.builders.org.uk

National Federation of Roofing
Contractors
Roofing House
31 Worship Street
London
EC2A 2DY
Tel: 020 7638 7663
www.nfrc.co.uk

National Institute of Carpet &
Floorlayers (NICF)
4c St Mary's Place
The Lace Market
Nottingham
NG1 1PH
Tel: 0115 958 3077
www.nicfltd.org.uk

Painting and Decorating Association
32 Coton Road
Nuneaton
Warwickshire
CV11 5TW
Tel: 024 7635 3776
www.paintingdecoratingassociation.
co.uk

Scottish and Northern Ireland Plumbing
Federation (SNIPEF)
2 Walker Street
Edinburgh
EH3 7LB
Tel: 0131 225 2255
www.snipef.org.uk

TrustMark
Englemere
Kings Ride
Ascot
Berkshire
SL5 7TB
Tel: 01344 630 804
www.trustmark.org.uk

Women and Manual Trades (WAMT)
52-54 Featherstone Street
London
EC1Y 8RT
Tel: 020 7251 9192
www.wamt.org

PROFESSIONALS

Accountants

Institute of Bookkeepers
1 Northumberland Avenue
Trafalgar Square
London
WC2N 5BW
Tel: 0845 060 2345
www.bookkeepers.org.uk

Association of Chartered Certified
Accountants in England and Wales
29 Lincoln's Inn Fields
London
WC2A 3EE
Tel: 0207 059 5000
www.accaglobal.com

Institute of Chartered Accountants in
England and Wales
PO Box 433
Moorgate Place
London
EC2P 2BJ
www.icaew.co.uk

Institute of Chartered Accountants in
Ireland
CA House, 83 Pembroke Road
Dublin 4
Republic of Ireland
Tel: (00 353) 1 637 7200
www.icai.ie

Institute of Chartered Accountants in
Scotland
CA House, 21 Haymarket Yards
Edinburgh
EH12 5BH
Tel: 0131 347 0100
www.icas.org.uk

Architects

Architects Registration Board (ARB)
8 Weymouth Street
London
W1W 5BU
Tel: 020 7580 5861
www.arb.org.uk

Royal Incorporation of Architects in
Scotland (RIAS)
15 Rutland Square
Edinburgh
EH1 2BE
Tel: 0131 229 7545
www.rias.org.uk

Royal Institute of British Architects
(RIBA)
66 Portland Place
London
W1B 1AD
Tel: 0207 580 5533
www.architecture.com

Royal Society of Architects in Wales
(RSAW)
4 Cathedral Road
Cardiff
CF11 9LJ
Tel: 029 2022 8989
www.architecture.com

Royal Society of Ulster Architects
(RSUA)
www.rsua.org.uk
2 Mount Charles
Belfast
BT7 1NZ
Tel: 028 9032 3760
www.rsua.org.uk

Estate agents

National Association of Estate Agents
(NAEC)
Arbon House
6 Tournament Court
Edgehill Drive
Warwick
Warwickshire
CV34 6LG
Tel: 01926 496800
www.naec.co.uk

The Property Ombudsman (TPO)
The Property Ombudsman
Beckett House
4 Bridge Street
Salisbury
Wiltshire SP1 2LX
Tel: 01722 333306
www.tpos.co.uk

**IFAs and other financial advisers
and brokers**

Financial Ombudsman Service (FOS)
South Quay Plaza
183 Marsh Wall
London
E14 9SR
Tel: 020 7964 1000
www.financial-ombudsman.org.uk

Financial Services Authority
25 The North Colonnade
Canary Wharf
London
E14 5HS
Tel: 020 7066 1000
www.fsa.gov.uk

Accountants

Institute of Bookkeepers
1 Northumberland Avenue
Trafalgar Square
London
WC2N 5BW
Tel: 0845 060 2345
www.bookkeepers.org.uk

Solicitors

The Law Society
113 Chancery Lane
London
WC2A 1PL
Tel: 020 7242 1222
www.lawsociety.org.uk

Legal Services Ombudsman
3rd Floor Sunlight House
Quay Street
Manchester
M3 3JZ
Tel: 0161 839 7262
www.olso.org

Northern Ireland Legal Services
2nd Floor
Waterfront Plaza
8 Laganbank Road
Mays Meadow
Belfast
BT1 3BN
Tel: 028 9040 8888
www.nilsc.org.uk

Solicitors Regulation Authority
Ipsley Court
Berrington Close
Redditch
B98 0TF
Tel: 0870 606 2555
www.sra.org.uk

Surveyors

Royal Institution of Chartered
Surveyors (RICS)
Parliament Square
London
SW1P 3AD
Tel: 0870 333 1600
www.rics.org

Surveyors Ombudsman Service
Tel: 0330 440 1634 or 01925 530 270
PO Box 1021
Warrington
WA4 9FE
www.surveyors-ombudsman.org.uk

MISCELLANEOUS TRADES

ACPO Secured by Design
1st Floor
10 Victoria Street
London
SW1H 0NN
Tel: 0207 084 8962
www.securedbydesign.com

Auto Locksmiths Association
Correspondence must be in writing to
the following:
The Committee
The Auto Locksmith Association
PO Box 66
Saxmundham
IP17 3WA

British Antique Furniture Restorer's
Association (BAFRA)
The Old Rectory
Warmwell
Dorchester
Dorset
DT2 8HQ
Tel: 01305 854822

British Association of Removers (BAR)
Tangent House
62 Exchange Road
Watford
Hertfordshire
WD18 0TG
Tel: 01923 699480
www.bar.co.uk

British Locksmiths Institute and Master
Locksmiths Association
5d Great Central Way
Woodford Halse
Daventry
Northants
NN11 3PZ
Tel: 01327 262 255
www.locksmiths.co.uk

The Guild of Master Sweeps
24 Church View
Aveley
Essex
RM15 4LH
Tel: 01953 455512
www.guild-of-master-sweeps.co.uk

Motor Codes Limited (Motor Industry
Code of Practice)
Forbes House
Halkin Street
London
SW1X 7DA
Tel: 0800 692 0825
www.motorindustrycodes.co.uk

National Association of Chimney
Sweeps (NACS)
Unit 15 Emerald Way
Stone Business Park
Stone
Staffordshire
ST15 0SR
Tel: 01785 811732
www.chimneyworks.co.uk

National Guild of Removers and Storers
PO Box 690
Chesham
Bucks
HP5 1WR
Tel:01494 792279
www.ngrs.co.uk

Pianoforte Tuners' Association (PTA)
P O Box 1312
Lightwater
Woking
GU18 5UB
Tel: 0845 602 8796
www.pianotuner.org.uk

Removals Industry Ombudsman
Service
Chess Chambers
2 Broadway Court
Chesham
Buckinghamshire
HP5 1EG
Tel: 01442 891736
www.removalsombudsman.org.uk

Retail Motor Industry Federation (RMIF)
201 Great Portland Street
London
W1W 5AB
Tel: 020 7580 6376
www.rmif.co.uk

The Trading Standards Institute and itsa
Limited
1 Sylvan Court
Sylvan Way
Southfields Business Park
Basildon
Essex
SS15 6TH
Tel: 08454 04 05 06
www.tradingstandards.gov.uk

General

Chartered Institute of Arbitrators
12 Bloomsbury Square
London
WC1A 2LP
Tel: 020 7421 7444
www.arbitrators.org

Citizens Advice Bureau
Myddelton House
115-123 Pentonville Road,
London
N1 9LZ
www.citizensadvice.org.uk

Consumer Direct
1 Victoria Street
London
SW1H 0ET
Tel: 08454 04 05 06
www.consumerdirect.gov.uk

HM Courts website
Customer Service Unit
Post Post 1.40
1st Floor
102 Petty France
London
SW1H 9AJ
Tel: 0845 4568770
www.hmcourts-service.gov.uk

Which? Legal Service
Tel: 01992 822 828
www.whichlegalservice.co.uk

Which? Local
www.which-local.co.uk

Index

Which? is the leading independent consumer champion in the UK.
A not-for-profit organisation, we exist to make individuals as powerful as the organisations they deal with in everyday life. The next few pages give you a taster of our many products and services. For more information, log onto www.which.co.uk or call 0800 252 100.

Which? magazine

Which? magazine has a simple goal in life – to offer truly independent advice to consumers that they can genuinely trust, from which credit card to use through to which washing machine to buy. Every month the magazine is packed with 84 advertisement-free pages of expert advice on the latest products. It takes on the biggest of businesses on behalf of all consumers and is not afraid to tell consumers to avoid their products. Truly the consumer champion. To subscribe, go to www.which.co.uk.

Which? online

www.which.co.uk gives you access to all Which? content online and much, much more. It's updated regularly, so you can read hundreds of product reports and Best Buy recommendations, keep up to date with Which? campaigns, compare products, use our financial planning tools and search for the best cars on the market. You can also access reviews from *The Good Food Guide*, register for email updates and browse our online shop – so what are you waiting for? To subscribe, go to www.which.co.uk.

Which? Local

Using a trader can be a bit hit and miss. But using one who's been recommended can help ensure a more reliable service. Which? Local is an easy to use website with thousands of recommendations for local traders across the UK reviewed by Which? members. From plumbers to builders, tree surgeons to hairdressers, Which? Local's listings have saved members time and money. If you're already a Which? member or want to find out more, visit www.which-local. co.uk. To find out how you can become a member call 01992 822 800.

Which? Computing

If you own a computer, are thinking of buying one or just want to keep abreast of the latest technology and keep up with your kids, there's one invaluable source of information you can turn to – *Which? Computing* magazine. *Which? Computing* offers you honest, unbiased reviews of new technology, problem-solving tips from the experts and step-by-step guides to help you make the most of your computer. To subscribe, go to www.which.co.uk.

Which? Money

Whether you want to boost your pension, make your savings work harder or simply need to find the best credit card, *Which? Money* has the information you need. *Which? Money* offers you honest, unbiased reviews of the best (and worst) new personal finance deals, from bank accounts to loans, credit cards to savings accounts. Throughout the magazine you will find tips and ideas to make your budget go further plus dozens of Best Buys. To subscribe, go to www.which.co.uk.

Which? Books

Which? Books provide impartial, expert advice on everyday matters from finance to law, property and major life events. We also publish the country's most trusted restaurant guide, *The Good Food Guide*. To find out more about Which? Books, log on to www.which.co.uk or call 01903 828557.

Wills & Probate
David Bunn
987-1-84490-070-1
Price £10.99

The best-selling guide to wills and applying for probate has been fully revised and updated to cover all of the latest changes to the Inheritance Tax laws. Providing expert, step-by-step advice on how to make a will, the pitfalls to avoid and what to do should you be called upon to wind up an estate, *Wills & Probate* is packed with jargon-free guidance on valuing and distributing assets, tackling official forms, timings, and what to expect. It also includes an exclusive discount for the Which? Wills online service.

Develop Your Property
Kate Faulkner
978-1-84490-038-1
Price £10.99

Develop Your Property gives you advice from the ground up. It looks at different methods to secure finance for your projects, what the typical costs for a conversion or extension might be and how to project-manage the critical details. Presenting the essential aspects of property development in a jargon-free and unbiased way, *Develop Your Property* will help you make the most of your biggest asset.

Pension Handbook
Jonquil Lowe
978-1-84490-025-1
Price £9.99
A definitive guide to sorting out your pension, whether you are deliberating over SERPs/S2Ps, organising a personal pension or moving schemes. Cutting through confusion and dispelling apathy, Jonquil Lowe provides expert advice on how to maximise your savings and provide for the future.

Divorce and Splitting Up
Imogen Clout
978-1-84490-034-3
Price £10.99
Divorce, separation, dissolution of a civil partnership or simply splitting up with a partner is never easy – the emotional upheaval, legal complexities and financial implications make even the most amicable parting a demanding business; when children are involved, couples are in dispute and property needs to be divided the whole process can be fraught with difficulties. *Divorce and Splitting Up* offers comprehensive, clear, step-by-step guidance through the whole process, explaining how the law works, drawing attention to key considerations and looking at ways of minimising unnecessary conflict and costs.

Save and Invest
Jonquil Lowe
978-1-84490-044-2
Price £10.99
Save and Invest is a detailed guide to all saving and investment avenues suitable for those approaching the markets for the first time and those seeking to improve their portfolio. Jonquil Lowe, an experienced investment analyst, introduces the basics of understanding risk and suggests popular starter investments. Many types of savings accounts are closely analysed, along with more complex investment options, such as venture capital trusts, high-income bonds, hedge funds and spread betting.

Don't get ripped off! Join Which? Legal Service and get 15 months' membership for the price of 12. Offer closes 30 June 2011.

Which? Legal Service offers unlimited expert legal advice by phone and email at an affordable price. If you've had poor service from a builder, bought faulty goods or you have problems with returning unwanted items, we can help you better understand your rights, to make sure you don't get ripped off.

As a member, you can call us Monday to Friday, 8.30am–6pm or email whenever it suits you – there is no limit to the number of times you can contact us. You can also access Which? Local to search online for local traders as recommended by Which? members.

To join Which? Legal Service, call 01992 822828 and quote LEGBB51.